RAND

U.S. Government Funding for Science and Technology Cooperation with Russia

Caroline Wagner, Irene Brahmakulam,
D. J. Peterson, Linda Staheli, Anny Wong

Prepared for the
Office of Science and Technology Policy

Science and Technology Policy Institute

The research described in this report was conducted by RAND's Science and Technology Policy Institute for the Office of Science and Technology Policy under Contract ENG-9812731.

ISBN: 0-8330-3145-7

Published 2002 by RAND
1700 Main Street, P.O. Box 2138, Santa Monica, CA 90407-2138
1200 South Hayes Street, Arlington, VA 22202-5050
201 North Craig Street, Suite 102, Pittsburgh, PA 15213
RAND URL: http://www.rand.org/
To order RAND documents or to obtain additional information, contact Distribution Services: Telephone: (310) 451-7002; Fax: (310) 451-6915; Email: order@rand.org

Preface

This document details U.S. government spending on cooperative science and technology (S&T) activities with Russian partners. The analysis was conducted at the request of the White House Office of Science and Technology Policy. The material is intended to provide information that will enrich decisionmaking about future cooperative ventures with Russia. It builds upon analysis conducted in earlier studies, including *International Cooperation in Research and Development: An Update to an Inventory of U.S. Government Spending*, RAND, MR-1248, 2000.

The project team received guidance from Dr. Gerald Hane (November 2000 until January 2001) and Dr. Amy Flatten (January 2001 onward), in the White House Office of Science and Technology Policy's National Security and International Affairs Division.

Created by Congress in 1991 as the Critical Technologies Institute, the Science and Technology Policy Institute was renamed in 1998. The Institute is a federally funded research and development center sponsored by the National Science Foundation and managed by RAND. The Institute's mission is to help improve public policy by conducting objective, independent research and analysis on policy issues that involve science and technology. To this end, the Institute

- supports the Office of Science and Technology Policy and other Executive Branch agencies, offices, and councils
- helps science and technology decisionmakers understand the likely consequences of their decisions and choose among alternative policies
- improves understanding in both the public and private sectors of the ways in which science and technology can better serve national objectives.

In carrying out its mission, the Institute consults broadly with representatives from private industry, institutions of higher education, and other nonprofit institutions.

Inquiries regarding the S&T Policy Institute or this document may be directed to:

Helga Rippen
Director, Science and Technology Policy Institute
1200 South Hayes Street
Arlington, VA 22202
Phone: 703-413-1100, ext. 5351
Web: http://www.rand.org/scitech/stpi
Email: stpi@rand.org

Contents

Figures

Tables

Summary

The United States government spent, on average, $350 million a year in the 1990s to support science and technology (S&T) cooperation with Russia. The amount rose in the early 1990s, peaked in 1996, and then began dropping in the late 1990s. When aggregated by dollars spent, the areas most likely to be the subject of cooperation are aerospace and aeronautical projects, engineering research, energy, and earth sciences. When counted by the number of projects (rather than funds committed), earth sciences—including geology, ocean studies, and atmospheric sciences—account for the largest number.

Earlier RAND studies suggested that, during the mid-1990s, cooperation with Russia claimed more government research and development (R&D) dollars than any other country. In order to examine the relationship in more detail, RAND collected and analyzed data at the project level and surveyed agency officials about specific projects and programs. These data were aggregated into categories created by RAND. This report provides an analytic, cross-agency overview, presenting a broad picture of the U.S.-Russia S&T relationship between 1994 and 1999.

The S&T relationship between the United States and Russia grew during the 1990s for reasons both scientific and political. Scientific reasons included the opening up of Russian institutes to greater international collaboration, offering unprecedented opportunities for joint work. Political reasons included the many complex factors involved in transitioning formerly defense-oriented Russian research centers to civilian activities.

The scientific and political motivations influence the types of spending that the U.S. government has committed to its relationship with Russia. Three types of spending can be distinguished as: (1) research and development funds; (2) mission-oriented support; and (3) policy-directed activities. Although these categories are not exclusive, they broadly characterize the type of activities being sponsored with Russia. Each type of spending represents a different mission of the U.S. government.

- Research and development projects (part of the $80 billion allocated within the federal budget to "R&D") are subject to merit-based, peer-reviewed scrutiny and are judged to be "good science." These activities generally are not aimed specifically at helping Russia, even though that may be a result.

- Mission-oriented science and technology support consists of funds (not budgeted as "R&D") spent by agencies to maintain a scientific or technological mission, to meet specific humanitarian or development goals, or to achieve a policy goal. These activities are sometimes aimed specifically at aiding Russia, and the majority of these funds are spent in or transferred to Russia.

- Policy-directed activities are determined by either the executive or legislative branches to be important for reaching a specific national security or environmental goal; some of these activities include a scientific or technical component. These funds are often aimed specifically at aiding Russia.

Different types of activities characterize the U.S.-Russia S&T relationship. These include (1) joint projects at the scientist-to-scientist level, (2) technical support provided by a U.S. agency for a counterpart agency or institute in Russia, (3) cooperative development of a database, (4) joint conferences or other scientific meetings, and (5) efforts to transfer Russian technology to the United States. Of the funds committed from the $80 billion R&D budget, the majority is spent on the first type: *joint projects* between scientists working toward a common research goal. These projects averaged $200 million a year between 1994 and 1999.

The percentage *share* of spending on joint projects is lower than it is with other scientifically advanced countries because the U.S. government has invested in types 2 through 5 (technical support activities, technology transfer, database development, and other forms of cooperation) at rates *higher than* with other countries. Technical support projects averaged nearly $90 million a year in the 1990s (dropping only slightly to $88 million in 1999 as overall spending dropped), compared with less than the $10 million that might be spent in our bilateral relationship with Canada or the United Kingdom. Database development projects reached $11 million in its highest year, and technology transfer claimed as much as $6.5 million in one year—compared with the $5 million that might be spent on such activities with other scientifically advanced countries.

For the most part, U.S. government investments in these activities were made without reference to Russia's investment. Russia's budget crisis has taken a toll on S&T funding, and many areas of Russian science are reportedly receiving less than they did in the mid-1990s. Nevertheless, in cases of collaborative research, U.S.-based scientists told us that their Russian counterparts provided a significant contribution to joint work. Most of this assistance has come as in-kind contributions, such as research experiments conducted in Russia labs or assistance to U.S. scientists in acquiring permits and other documentation. In addition, Russian partners have provided invaluable access to data and resources, according to U.S. scientists. Although Russian financial contributions did not equal that of the United States, scientists reported that the joint work could not have been done without Russian collaboration.

Overall, the U.S. government's projects with Russia take on a slightly different pattern than can be observed with other scientifically advanced countries. Among S&T partners, U.S.-Russian S&T cooperation is

- more binational in character than is the case between the United States and other scientifically advanced countries (i.e., a smaller percentage of funds are spent on multinational activities)

- less collaborative than with other countries (i.e., a smaller *percentage* of activities involve scientist-to-scientist interaction)

- more technology-based (research with other countries is more science-based)

- less of a shared effort than is the case with other advanced countries (the United States is putting more funding into the relationship than is Russia)

- more often taking place in Russia than is the case with other countries

- dominated by spending in aerospace applications.

To understand the extent to which Russia may be contributing to joint S&T activities, we examined budget data and policy statements about Russian S&T activities. We found that U.S. government investments in the binational relationship are strongly correlated to Russian S&T priorities in four areas: (1) biomedical and health sciences, (2) energy, (3) engineering, and (4) physics. This suggests that U.S. investments may provide fertile ground for joint work in these areas. A common emphasis on defense sciences, environment and earth sciences, ocean studies, and materials sciences also suggests that cooperation in these fields may be productive and useful for both sides. In contrast, the United States is making investments in geology, seismology, and social sciences even as Russian R&D funding is relatively weak in these fields, suggesting that perhaps U.S. investment in these areas is not being matched by Russia in any meaningful way. A funding gap between strong Russian investment and weak U.S. investment in several R&D areas suggests that cooperation could be enhanced in the fields of chemistry, construction, information technologies, telecommunications, and transportation.

Similar opportunities for joint work may exist in several areas where the Russian government has set aside funds for international cooperation, and where the

United States is not making a significant investment. These areas are mining, agricultural genetics, and earth sciences.

Five agencies of government provide nearly 90 percent of the funding for the joint R&D relationship: the National Aeronautic and Space Administration, the Department of Energy, the Department of Health and Human Services, the National Science Foundation, and the Department of Defense. Agencies funding other mission-oriented science and technology support activities are led by the U.S. Agency for International Development, followed by the Department of Agriculture, the Department of State, and a number of smaller government agencies. Although mission-oriented S&T spending is concentrated in these eight agencies, as many as 18 federal agencies are sponsoring S&T projects with Russia.

Reports from scientists working with Russian counterparts indicate that the United States is gaining significant scientific benefit from working with Russian counterparts. While agency officials reported that funding for the U.S.-Russia S&T relationship seems to have dropped in 2001, there has been a revived interest within the U.S. scientific community in working with Russia and an increase in the number of projects being considered has been observed. Nevertheless, significant administrative obstacles to working with Russia remain. As Russian science continues to be restructured, we expect that funding patterns will change over time to look more like the U.S. relationship with other scientifically advanced countries.

Abbreviations

BTEP	Biotechnology Engagement Program
CDC	Centers for Disease Control and Prevention
CERN	European Organization for Nuclear Research
CRDF	Civilian Research and Development Foundation
CTR	Cooperative Threat Reduction
DOC	Department of Commerce
DOD	Department of Defense
DOE	Department of Energy
EPA	Environmental Protection Agency
FEMA	Federal Emergency Management Agency
FSU	Former Soviet Union
HIV/AIDS	Human Immunodeficiency Virus/Acquired Immunodeficiency Syndrome
HHS	Department of Health and Human Services
IPP	Initiatives for Proliferation Prevention program
ISTC	The International Science and Technology Center
ISTA	International Science and Technology Agreement
ITER	International Thermonuclear Experimental Reactor
MOC	Memorandum of cooperation
MOU	Memorandum of understanding
NASA	National Aeronautics and Space Administration
NCI	Nuclear Cities Initiative
NIH	National Institutes of Health
NIS	Newly Independent States
NOAA	National Oceanic and Atmospheric Administration
NRC	Nuclear Regulatory Commission
NSF	National Science Foundation
R&D	Research and development
RaDiUS	Research and Development in the United States
S&T	Science and technology

STD	Sexually transmitted disease
USAID	United States Agency for International Development
USDA	United States Department of Agriculture
USDA/ARS	USDA Agricultural Research Service
USDA/ERS	USDA Economic Research Service
USDA/FAS	USDA Foreign Agriculture Service
USDA/NASS	USDA National Agricultural Statistics Services
USGS	United States Geological Survey
WHO	World Health Organization

1. Introduction: U.S. Government Funding of Science and Technology Cooperation with Russia

A strong system of higher education coupled with robust support for research in the natural sciences, social sciences, and humanities is a prerequisite for successful political and economic transitions in Russia.

—An Agenda for Renewal
Carnegie Endowment for International Peace,
2000

During the 1990s, international science and technology (S&T) cooperation increased worldwide. The National Science Board reports that, betweeen 1987 and 1997, the number of science and technology articles that were internationally co-authored doubled to account for 15 percent of all articles published (NSB, 2000). U.S. government funding for international cooperation in S&T (hereafter, "cooperation") also grew. In 1997,[1] cooperation accounted for about 6 percent of the federal research and development (R&D) budget, up from 4 percent in 1995 (Wagner, Yezril, and Hassell, 2000).

The S&T relationship between the United States and Russia also grew in the 1990s. U.S. cooperation with Russia grew for both scientific and political reasons. Scientific reasons included the opening of Russian scientific institutes to greater international cooperation, offering unprecedented opportunities for joint work.[2] In addition, a number of political reasons motivated the significant growth in the S&T relationship. These included the strategic need to help former weapons scientists transition to civilian R&D and to encourage them to remain in Russia, the need to aid in dismantling weapons of mass destruction, and the need to strengthen the Russian economy to help bolster social and political order. Although political considerations play a role in international S&T projects sponsored with other countries, U.S. government support for the S&T relationship with Russia displays an even greater interweaving of scientific and political motivations.

---

[1]Unless otherwise noted, all dates in this report represent fiscal year spending (October 1–September 30). All spending is reported in then U.S. dollars.

[2]An index of scientific capacity, developed by RAND, parses countries of the world into four groups representing levels of scientific capacity. Russia is among the group of 25 scientifically advanced countries. See Wagner et al. (2001).

Earlier RAND research found that when spending is examined on a binational basis—where the United States is working with just one other country—Russia came up at the top of the list during the 1990s (Wagner, Yezril, and Hassell, 2000). As a result of this research, it became clear that the U.S. government's funding for the S&T relationship with Russia is not well documented. Accordingly, we set out to examine the relationship in more detail and, in particular, to detail as much as possible the "bottom-up" relationship being forged by individual scientists.

RAND collected and analyzed data on project-level R&D spending and aggregated this into different categories. We also collected information on S&T programs designed specifically to aid Russian science. This report is an analytic, cross-agency overview, presenting a broad picture of the U.S.-Russia S&T relationship between 1994 and 1999. It seeks to complement other reviews that examine the relationship from political and strategic perspectives.[3] The value-added of this study is that, unlike other reports, the data are presented as a cross-section of agency activity, and they are aggregated from the bottom up: We start with actual scientific activities and collate this information into categories that are not otherwise available.

It is important to note that this study does not address the question of whether the spending has been effective in reaching political or even scientific goals. There are many measures of effectiveness, and even if they had been applied in this case, judging success is subjective and qualitative. This report is designed to provide quantitative data about U.S. government spending on cooperation with Russia; we hope that the data will aid decisionmakers in examining the trends and the overall effectiveness of spending on the U.S.-Russia S&T relationship. Although we made an effort to find corresponding data from Russian sources to compare with our findings, the data available are not directly comparable. Additional research will be needed to find out how much the Russian government commits to cooperative S&T activities.

Organization of This Report

Following this introduction, Section 2 puts into context the U.S. government contribution to the S&T relationship with Russia by describing motivations for as well as the types of spending committed to the relationship. Section 3 presents data on U.S. government R&D spending. Section 4 reports on mission-oriented

---

[3]For example, the State Department has published a comprehensive review. See U. S. Department of State (2001).

and policy-directed S&T activities, including special programs supporting the relationship with Russia. Section 5 summarizes the observations of U.S. scientists who have worked with counterparts in Russia. Appendix A presents a summary table of U.S. government spending on the S&T relationship by agency. Appendix B presents a detailed methodology used for creating the data and analysis in this report. Appendix C lists the U.S.-Russia S&T agreements collected by the Department of State and available at the time this report was printed. Appendix D presents the questions used for discussions with U.S. scientists. The bibliography suggests additional reading.

Methodology and Definitions Used in This Report

We consulted a number of sources to compile information and analyze the U.S.-Russia S&T relationship. Some information on government R&D spending is electronically available through RAND's RaDiUS database (http://radius.rand.org). RaDiUS is a fully searchable data system that contains information on the more than $80 billion of annual spending (in fiscal year 1999)[4] classified by the federal government as "research and development."[5] We used RaDiUS in the first stage of data collection. We also consulted existing literature, including government policy documents, for information on the overall U.S.-Russian S&T relationship. We queried government agencies, and a number of them provided program descriptions and funding information to RAND. To get a richer picture of the relationship, we also conducted a series of conversations with U.S. scientists who have worked with Russian counterparts.

Terms such as "S&T" and "R&D" are used in this report to put spending into context for the reader and, in particular, for government policymakers who wish to have an overview of the full S&T relationship. These are not exclusive categories: R&D spending could certainly be considered "science" in the broad sense. Spending within special projects—those not budgeted as R&D, such as the Civilian Research and Development Fund—include activities that scientists call "research and development." The categories are presented here, and activities are classified into either R&D or S&T, because these are the terms and budget categories that the U.S. government uses to define different kinds of spending.

---

[4]Only those activities classified by federal agencies as "R&D" are included in this inventory. Joint scientific and technological projects, not counted as R&D, will be described later in this report. The funds spent on R&D are described each year in a publication issued by the American Association for the Advancement of Science. The most recent of these documents is *Congressional Action on Research and Development in the FY2001 Budget*, Washington, D.C.: AAAS, 2001.

[5]"Research and development" is a budget term used by the Office of Management and Budget and applied within government agencies to define a specific form of federal investment activity. (For more on this, see Appendix B.)

Characterizing the relationship according to government budget categories makes it possible to examine the relationship in more detail. Admittedly, this could be confusing for the reader because we use the term "S&T" to apply to the whole set of activities as well as to a subset of agency programs within the overall relationship. We have made every effort to be as clear as possible when using the terms so that the reader can follow these distinctions. However, we acknowledge that this is not always easy.

Because of the way the government budgets for and spends money, it is often difficult to decouple international activities from other parts of government spending. As a result, we include in this study any type of program-based activity that has, as *one of the principal purposes*, the sponsorship of cooperation with Russia, or where multinational projects involve Russia as a partner. The inclusion of a project in this inventory does not mean that the spending took place in Russia. In fact, more than half of the spending appears to have taken place in the United States. We included a project when, as part of its activities, scientists between the two countries actively cooperated with each other.

It is important to keep in mind that the activities reported here represent what might be called "formal cooperation," where cooperation is a stated goal and an operating principle. The amounts reported understate the full extent of cooperation, since scientists and engineers often share information with counterparts in other countries in the course of conducting scientific research.

For the purpose of this study, a number of common terms are used, and it is important to be clear how they are being used in this report:

- *Science and technology* refers to the many different investments made by the U.S. government in basic research, in applied research, in development of equipment and standards, and in data collection and analysis needed both to increase knowledge about the natural world and to help the U.S. government in its various missions.

- *Research and development* is a subset of S&T activities. The term refers to programs and projects budgeted as "research and development" by federal agencies. These generally are activities that seek to apply the scientific method to specific experimental questions identified by government agencies as important and validated by scientific peers as worthwhile.

- *Curiosity-driven research* is the set of S&T activities that are proposed by scientists and conducted, usually as basic research, because the subject is not well understood and where the application of the scientific method of observation and experimentation may add to the stock of knowledge.

- *Mission-oriented research* is the set of S&T activities that are defined by government agency officials to commission or conduct research, usually applied research or development, that will advance knowledge needed for an agency to carry out its mission.

- *Policy-oriented research* is the set of S&T activities that are defined by government officials or elected representatives to reach a policy-oriented goal using S&T as a tool.

- *Cooperation* refers to all the programs, projects, and support activities sponsored by the U.S. government with Russia that have a scientific or technical component. It can include joint R&D, technical assistance, technology transfer, standards development, and other types of joint activities.

2. Science and Technology Cooperation in Context

The U.S. government actively supports and participates in international S&T. In 1997, the U.S. government spent more than $4.4 billion to support formal cooperative activities, ranging from huge multinational "megascience" projects like the International Space Station to small grants that fund research experiments conducted by U.S. scientists in cooperation with their counterparts in other countries. Other activities include assistance projects such as those helping to develop a pest-resistant strain of wheat for Central American farms, monitoring of the global atmosphere, or seeking the causes of infectious disease. International cooperation in research and development amounts to about 6 percent of the U.S. federal R&D budget (Wagner, Yezril, and Hassell, 2001).

In addition to spending on international R&D, the government also funds other activities that have a scientific or technological component and that involve international coordination or cooperation. These activities include weather tracking, mapping, seismic detection, and space and defense operations. In 1997, mission-oriented activities accounted for perhaps as much as $1 billion of U.S. government spending over and above the funds committed from the R&D budget.

With only a few exceptions,[1] the U.S. government does not fund international S&T activities for their own sake: Collaborative activities usually build scientific capabilities that are central to scientific or national interests or that meet mission-specific requirements. Accordingly, international activities are not budgeted separately or in a manner that can be easily identified and tracked. Determining how these funds are being spent requires analysts to review descriptions of thousands of individual programs, projects, and awards and to interview government officials. Even within specific programs and projects, it is often difficult to decouple international activities from other parts of the programs. As a result, we include in this study any type of program-based activity that has, as *one of the principal purposes*, the sponsorship of cooperation with Russian partners.

---

[1] At least two R&D agencies have offices designed to coordinate and encourage international linkages. The Fogarty Center at the National Institutes of Health spends R&D funds to facilitate international exchange, and the Office of International Programs at the National Science Foundation provides assistance to existing collaborations to aid with travel or conferencing requirements.

Diverse Government Activities Create the S&T Relationship

In order to put into context the U.S. government's spending on S&T cooperation with Russia, it is important to understand how the government budgets for and allocates funding. S&T spending on the bilateral relationship can be divided into three categories: curiosity-driven R&D, mission-oriented support, and policy-directed activities.

The distinction between funds spent on curiosity-driven R&D and those supporting mission-oriented S&T or policy-directed activities is not transparent to those examining U.S. government activities. Nevertheless, the differences are important because they affect the allocation, spending, and evaluation of government programs. These categories are described briefly below.

Curiosity-Driven R&D

Curiosity-driven R&D is the most widely referenced category within which cooperation takes place: A significant amount of federal discretionary spending is budgeted as R&D. According to the president's budget, the funds budgeted in 1999 as R&D totaled more than $80 billion. This included a good portion of the budgets of the National Science Foundation (NSF), the National Institutes of Health (NIH), the Department of Energy (DOE), and the Department of Defense (DOD). Many of the dollars committed as curiosity-driven R&D are administered by government agencies in the form of grants given directly to U.S.-based scientists on a competitive basis on the merit of their proposals. Curiosity-driven R&D is shown in Figure 2.1 as the numerous "bottom-up" arrows.

Curiosity-driven R&D funds are administered through a peer-review process based on scientific merit. For the most part, the funding for these projects is provided to U.S. scientists who in turn collaborate with Russian counterparts. Funds are usually not provided to the foreign collaborator. These projects are not conducted explicitly to aid Russia, even if this is one result. The projects are funded because the research has been judged by peers to advance knowledge and understanding. In many cases, the projects could not be done without collaborating with Russian experts or accessing Russian-based resources or data. These projects are similar to ones conducted by U.S. scientists with counterparts in countries around the world.

U.S. spending that involves cooperation with Russia on curiosity-driven R&D is described in Section 3.

Mission-Oriented Support

Agencies also commit resources to S&T activities that support their missions. Examples are weather data collected by the National Oceanographic and Atmospheric Administration (NOAA); mapping and fish and wildlife tracking by the Department of the Interior; and pest management by the Department of Agriculture (USDA). Mission-oriented support also includes direct assistance funds such as those spent by the U.S. Agency for International Development (USAID) and the Department of State.

Mission-oriented support is committed in various ways. Contracts are often used to fund laboratory operations, data collection and analysis efforts, and humanitarian and developments programs. These types of funds are represented in Figure 2.1 as the large arrows on the left. The funds can be both bottom-up, in the sense that they are committed to support merit-based scientific research—such as installing seismological equipment—or they can be top-down, in the sense that they are dedicated to a specific mission such as aiding the Russian health sector. In some cases, funds are provided directly to Russian researchers, although most of the funding is provided to U.S. researchers who, in turn, collaborate with Russian counterparts. Mission-oriented support is more difficult to track because, unlike R&D, the funds are not tagged and identified separately within the federal budget. Mission-oriented support programs with Russia are described in Section 4.

Policy-Directed Cooperation

The federal government runs programs and undertakes projects that contribute to political or strategic missions and whose actualization may include S&T. In the case of Russia, several programs have been put into place over the past decade specifically to enhance both R&D opportunities and the greater S&T cooperative relationship. These include the Civilian Research and Development Foundation (CRDF) and the International Science and Technology Center (ISTC). These projects are undertaken, not because they serve a scientific or research mission even though this may be a result, but because the government has other important goals. Science and technology are tools to help reach these goals. This does not mean that good science is not being conducted within these programs: Calling the cooperation "policy-directed" is simply a way to understand the motivating factor behind the government's commitment of funds.

Funds dedicated to policy-directed activities are committed in several ways: First, they are often directly appropriated by Congress and then budgeted within an agency, allocated to a program, and spent by a division as part of their operational budgets. A second way funds are committed is through a mission agency that seeks to reach a policy goal (such as disposition of nuclear materials) through cooperation. A third way funds are provided to these projects and programs lies outside of government: Nongovernmental organizations also commit funds to aid government-created programs, leveraging government investment and increasing the effectiveness of the spending by all parties. Often, these funds are provided directly to Russian scientists. Congressional action under the Freedom Support Act and the Cooperative Threat Reduction (CTR) program legislating activities to aid or otherwise work with Russia are examples of policy-directed activities.[2] These resources are represented in Figure 2.1 as the "down" arrows. Policy-directed S&T cooperation efforts are described in Section 4.

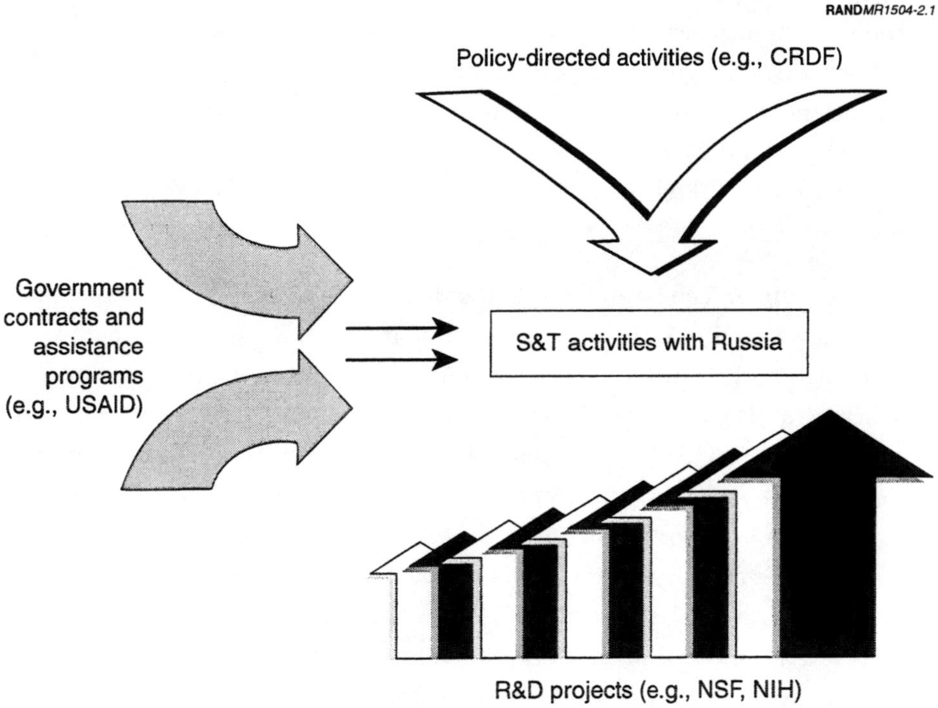

RAND*MR1504-2.1*

Figure 2.1—Government Missions and Roles Creating the S&T
Relationship with Russia

[2]Not included in this study are policy-directed technical assistance activities funded under the CTR program and the Nuclear Cities Initiative with goals such as nuclear reactor safety, materials protection, proliferation prevention, fissile materials disposition, and other disarmament programs.

The Role of Science and Technology Agreements

The U.S. government negotiates and signs formal and informal agreements to cooperate internationally in S&T. The political goals of national governments and the mission requirements of their agencies motivate these government-to-government agreements. Science and technology agreements, sometimes called International Science and Technology Agreements (ISTAs), range from legally binding treaties approved by Congress to letters of correspondence with no legally binding authority.

The U.S. government has signed both an executive-level "umbrella" ISTA and dozens of agency-level ISTAs with Russia. The umbrella ISTA, signed in 1993, remains in effect until December 2003. The Department of State reports that, additionally, there are 62 active ISTAs between the United States and Russia signed at the agency level. The subjects of the agreements range broadly in the areas they target. Environmental and earth sciences (14), aeronautics (8), and cooperation in general and basic science (7) claim the highest number of agreements. The agencies reporting the largest number of agreements with Russia are DOE (10), the National Aeronautics and Space Administration (NASA) (9), and the Department of Commerce (DOC) (7). Appendix A has a list of agency-level ISTAs signed with Russia, as reported by the Department of State.

S&T agreements can be an important indicator of national interest to cooperate in S&T. However, ISTAs are nonfunded, diplomatic-level agreements that have no associated budget authority. Many ISTAs are never fully implemented because of a lack of funds from one or both signatories. Sometimes, an agreement is made to cooperate and an ISTA is signed to establish the parameters of this cooperation. In other cases, S&T projects take place without reference to an ISTA. Relying on a list of ISTAs to provide a picture of the bilateral S&T relationship between the United States and any other country can be misleading when the goal is to identify the range and character of cooperation. Accordingly, although we include a list of U.S.-Russia ISTAs, this study presents actual funding of specific activities without regard to whether they are covered by an ISTA.

3. The Research and Development Relationship with Russia

Funding Levels

U.S. government spending on cooperative R&D with Russia averaged $322 million between 1994 and 1999. It rose in the early 1990s to a peak of about $380 million in 1996 and 1997 and then declined to about $275 million in 1999 (Figure 3.1).[1]

Research and development projects with Russia, like most R&D projects, are funded as part of a peer-reviewed, merit-based process. Because the criterion for funding R&D is based on the excellence of the scientific or technical proposal, the funds shown in Figure 3.1 cannot be interpreted as ones set aside to aid Russia. Moreover, this funding is not necessarily spent in Russia. Two broad modes of operation characterize international R&D activities: Either the R&D takes place in the United States and then the U.S.-based researcher coordinates or shares information with a Russian counterpart, or the research and data collection phase takes place in Russia and the data analysis is done in the United States. Based on interviews with scientists, we estimate that less than half of these funds were actually spent in Russia.

The bilateral R&D relationship is notable because the U.S. government funds projects that add up to more than double the funds it spends on cooperation with other countries (Wagner, Yezril, and Hassell, 2001). This large investment is likely due to several factors, some political and some scientific. On the political side, many in the West perceived that it was important to "save Russian science" given the rocky economic downturn and institutional reshuffling that accompanied the breakup of the Soviet Union.[2] In addition, the investment reflects the strategic needs of Western countries to ensure the security of the Russian nuclear weapons complex and the concomitant goals of retooling Russian defense engineering toward civilian applications. The quick rise in the investment may reflect the lack of a robust relationship between the two countries prior to 1990.

---

[1] This spending includes both bilateral and multilateral efforts with Russia.
[2] See Schweitzer (1997) and Boesman (1993).

12

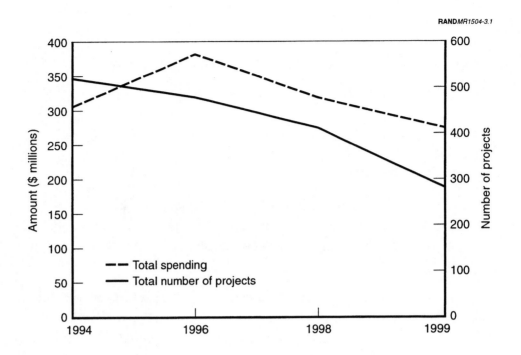

Figure 3.1—U.S.-Russia Bilateral and Multilateral Cooperative Research: Number of Projects and Spending, 1994–1999

On the scientific side, motivations for a larger combined program with Russia may include the unprecedented historical changes in the political organization of Russia in the early 1990s that created valuable new opportunities for scientific cooperation.[3] In addition, pollution problems and the needs within Russia for a more efficient energy sector created scientific imperatives for cooperation.

In an index of S&T capacity created by RAND in 2000, Russia ranked among the top 25 scientifically advanced countries, suggesting that significant unexploited potential for cooperation existed during the 1990s, and further suggesting that the large investment creating robust ties with Russia was a reasonable investment of R&D funds. Indeed, the share of jointly authored publications between U.S. and Russian scientists rose from less than 10 percent of all Russian

---

[3] A 2000 report detailing international linkages in science note the historically weak S&T linkages between the United States and Eastern European countries, a feature that suggests a potential for growth. See Zitt, Bassecoulard, and Okubo (2000). It should also be noted that historical analysis of Russian science is complicated by the shift from reporting on all of the Soviet Union prior to its 1991 breakup, to reporting on different independent states with varying S&T capacities. Even when data are collected as coming from the USSR, it can be assumed that the then Russian Soviet Federated Socialist Republic accounted for a good percentage of the activities. The actual percentages, however, are unknown.

publications in 1988 to 23 percent in 1997, which suggests that joint projects were productive (National Science Board, 2000).[4]

During the period studied, the share of R&D funding contributing to nonproliferation goals grew from about $23 million in 1994 to about $56 million in 1998. As shown in Figure 3.1, U.S. government spending on cooperative R&D with Russia peaked in 1996–1997 and then declined in 1998–1999. (There are preliminary indications that in 2000–2001 the amount of funding may have leveled out.) During this period, the number of projects also declined by almost 50 percent. These features of the relationship may be explained by several factors. First several major R&D activities were scaled back or phased out in the late 1990s, including the Mars-98 mission and U.S. participation in the International Thermonuclear Experimental Reactor (ITER)—both of which were expensive projects. This fact alone accounts for a significant portion of the drop in funding. In addition, the decline in the number of projects may be explained by the fact that, given the newness of R&D opportunities in Russia in the early 1990s, U.S. researchers and managers chose to develop smaller ventures as "phase-one" efforts, pilot projects, or feasibility studies; and they may have chosen to spread these opportunities across a large number of institutions and fields to test initial hypotheses and new relationships. As U.S. researchers' knowledge of Russian capabilities developed, and as the number of active researchers and competitive research institutions in Russia declined, efforts may have focused on the best institutions and researchers and the most promising opportunities. This winnowing process may have been accentuated by the general deterioration in the condition of the Russian R&D establishment and the decline in the number of Russian researchers active in the 1990s.

Another factor driving the changing level of activity in the 1990s may have been a change in the U.S. policy environment. Immediately after the breakup of the Soviet Union, U.S. political priorities directed significant support to Russia in an effort to encourage rapid economic and political change. The Freedom Support Act was a key element of this strategy. But in the mid-1990s, frustrations with the pace of change in Russia and questions about the efficacy of U.S. assistance efforts emerged. This resulted in a shifting of priorities and a reprogramming of resources in the late 1990s—first, by shifting some funds to the Ukraine and then further shifting funds to Central Asia and the Caucasus.

Finally, the reduction in the level of spending and the number of projects may also signal that, after several years of "making up for lost ground," Russia is

---

[4]It is important to note that data collected in the 1980s included all republics of the former Soviet Union. We accounted for this in the percentage share reported here.

coming to be considered more of a "normal" or "traditional" cooperative partner. Thus, bilateral activities are settling into patterns similar to those that characterize the U.S. relationship with other scientifically advanced countries. Although the number of projects and funding levels fell, scientists believe that the overall quality of the U.S.-Russia cooperative relationship may well have improved.

Types of R&D Cooperation

When grouped into types of activities, the majority of funds in each of the years examined were spent on joint R&D projects,[5] followed by technical support, database development, technology transfer, and a small amount of spending on standards development and conferences. Figure 3.2 illustrates the share of spending by type of activity (joint or collaborative research, technical support, and so on) for each of the four years examined. In comparison to the U.S.

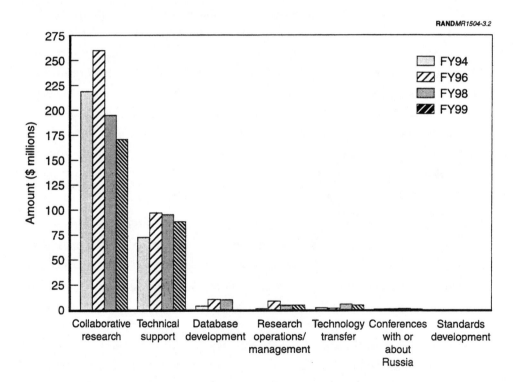

Figure 3.2—U.S.-Russia Cooperative Research by Type of Activity,
1994–1999

---

[5]This funding includes both bilateral and multilateral efforts with Russia.

government's relationship with other scientifically advanced countries, technology transfer and database development account for a larger share of the relationship.

Collaboration

U.S. government spending on joint research—where scientists work collaboratively with their counterparts in Russia toward a common scientific goal—averaged $200 million in the period studied. They peaked in 1996 at $260 million and dropped to $170 million in 1999 (Figure 3.3).[6] It is notable that, by the end of the 1990s, although the total amount of spending was higher than it was with other scientifically advanced countries, the *share* of U.S. government spending on collaboration with Russia was lower. As a general rule, joint, or "collaborative," research makes up 75 percent of spending between the United States and other scientifically advanced countries.

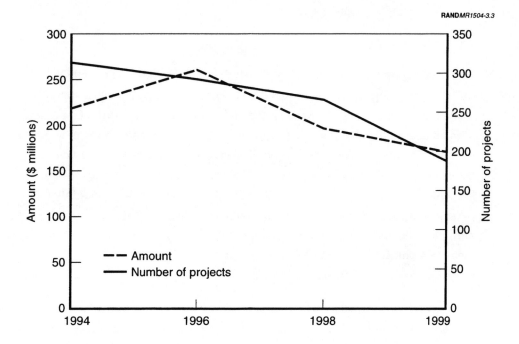

Figure 3.3—Number of Bilateral and Multilateral Collaborative Research Projects and Spending

---

[6]This study did not examine private or nongovernmental spending on cooperation with Russia; the patterns there may be quite different.

In the mid-1990s, this was also the case with Russia, but as funding declined in the late 1990s, the share of activities that involved collaborative research dropped faster than spending overall. By 1999, collaborative research accounted for 63 percent of all activities. The drop can partly be accounted for by the completion of some multimillion-dollar projects (totaling approximately $25 million) in aerospace, engineering, defense, and other physical sciences in 1998.

The joint research projects examined for this study represent a broad array of scientific and technical inquiry. Examples include

- comparative analysis of the Group A and B streptococcal genome, a collaborative undertaking by the Institute of Experimental Medicine in St. Petersburg and the University of Oklahoma Health Sciences Center, and

- establishment of an acoustic array to investigate large-scale changes in the Arctic Ocean temperature and scattering of underwater sound by sea ice, under a Gore-Chernomyrdin Memorandum of Agreement.

Technical Support

Technical support projects averaged nearly $90 million a year in the 1990s, dropping only slightly to $88.7 million in 1999 as overall spending dropped. This is about 25 percent of all the R&D spending identified for this study. Compared with other scientifically advanced countries, this is a high percentage of technical support. As noted above, U.S. cooperation with scientifically advanced countries heavily favors collaboration rather than technical support. The large amount of R&D funds going for technical support with Russia is more like cooperative patterns with scientifically developing countries (Wagner et al., 2001). For example, an earlier RAND study of cooperative research in North America found that U.S. technical support to Mexico accounted for 25 percent of R&D funds compared with the 5 percent committed to Canada (Wagner and Berstein, 1999).

All the activities funded by USAID are counted as technical support projects, as are well as over half of DOE's projects. Examples of technical support projects include

- U.S. technical assistance and support for energy efficiency and renewable energy activities, under the Russian-American Energy Efficiency work plan, in support of the Russian-American Memorandum of Cooperation for Energy Efficiency, and

- support and training to expand emergency response capabilities in Russia.

Technology Transfer

Although technology transfer is not a significant part of the U.S. relationship with most other scientifically advanced countries, the relationship with Russia is a notable counterexample. Technology transfer spending reached as much as $6.5 million—the amount of R&D money spent in 1998 to test and evaluate Russian technologies for U.S. use. (Recall that technology transfer involves U.S. efforts to seek technology that it could use to serve government missions.) During the period we studied, technology transfer rose from $2 million in 1994 to $6 million in 1999. Examples of technology transfer include DOD's procuring of Russian castings for more-affordable U.S. fighter structures, and DOE's initiating the transfer of Russian plutonium production reactor core conversion for U.S. use.

Database Development

Projects dedicated to evaluating data, compiling them into useable data sets, and developing new databases also claimed more U.S. funding than is the case with other scientifically advanced countries. Database development projects totaled as much as $11 million in 1996. In addition, conversations with scientists, described in Section 6, revealed a number of collaborative projects that also had the goal of developing databases as part of their research plans (these projects would not be counted toward the total "database development" funding). Much valuable data collected by Russian scientists have only been accessible since the breakup of the Soviet Union. It is fair to say that the task of accessing and evaluating data and building them into databases useable by the international scientific community was an important part of the relationship between the United States and Russia in the years we examined. Examples of databases include those developed for the International Space Station; for solar terrestrial surface radiation over the Arctic basin; and to index and track Russian biomedical articles and publications. Given that many Russian institutes have only recently joined the international scientific community, it is understandable that an effort to make their data widely available would have been an important part of activities in the 1990s.

Binational Versus Multinational Cooperation

U.S. scientists cooperating with Russian counterparts are more often involved in binational than multinational activities. An average of 75 percent of joint R&D with Russia is binational. The solid part of the bars in Figure 3.4 shows the share of funding that is dedicated to binational cooperation. It is clear that this is the

18

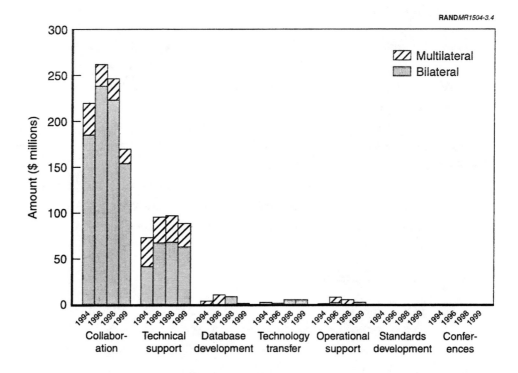

Figure 3.4—Shares of Binational and Multinational Cooperation by Type of Activity, 1994, 1996, 1998, and 1999

dominant form of shared activity across all types of cooperative projects. Multinational collaboration is a smaller percentage of activities in each category.

The share of binational versus multinational activities favors binational activities, more so than is the case in cooperation with other scientifically advanced countries. When spending on cooperation is examined by this measure, multinational cooperation is more likely to claim half or more of U.S. government spending with other scientifically advanced countries. For example, in earlier RAND research, we found that, across all cooperative R&D spending with Canada, 55 percent of U.S. government spending on cooperation involved multinational activities (Wagner and Berstein, 1999).

The dominance of binational activities may result from Russia's relatively late entry into the international scientific community. As a general rule, multinational research activities take many years to build. Partners negotiate for years on agreements and terms of reference surrounding cooperation; additional time is devoted to the design and execution of scientific research projects. For example, important international collaborative projects, such as the Human Frontiers Science Program and the Human Genome Project, began to form in the late 1980s and early 1990s before Russian scientists had actively joined the international scientific community.[7] Moreover, these international activities require an up-front financial commitment that has been difficult for Russia to make. As Russian scientists become more integrated into the world scientific community, we expect U.S. spending with Russia to become more multinational, a pattern similar to that of other scientifically advanced countries.

Fields of Science Represented

The U.S. government funds cooperation with Russia across a broad range of subjects. In a pattern similar to that seen with other scientifically advanced countries, joint projects in aerospace account for the largest amount of cooperative spending with Russia, followed by spending in engineering, energy, biomedical and health sciences, physics, and defense sciences. When viewed in terms of the number of projects conducted (not spending), the picture changes slightly. Excluding aerospace, there are more collaborative projects in the social sciences and the earth sciences (geology, oceanography) than in other areas.

Aerospace

In a pattern similar to that seen with other major collaborators, joint projects in aerospace account for the largest amount of spending by the U.S. government, averaging at least $170 million a year over the past decade. Large-scale, international NASA projects—where both sides contribute funding and know-how—account for a number of these projects. Figure 3.5 shows the dominance of aerospace projects in spending.

This pattern is similar to that seen with other scientifically advanced countries—spending on large aerospace projects often puts that field at the top of the list. Aerospace and related areas of science (e.g., aeronautics, space-related life sciences) dominated spending with Russia in each of the years examined. Nevertheless, the completion of several large missions means that spending in this area had dropped considerably, from $200 million in 1998 to $66 million in 1999.

International cooperation in aerospace generally involves no exchange of funds: In practice, U.S. researchers conduct work and then share data or combine equipment to meet an agreed-upon mission. Joint aerospace projects have included

---

[7]U.S. participation in these collaborative activities is the subject of Wagner et al., forthcoming.

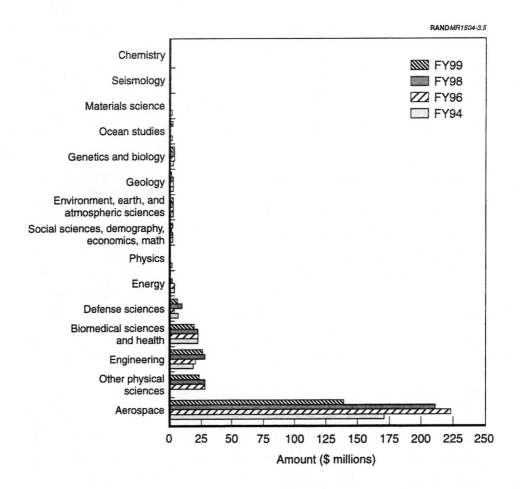

RAND*MR1504-3.5*

**Figure 3.5—Spending on Areas of S&T Cooperation by Field,
Including Aerospace, 1994, 1996, 1998, and 1999**

- sharing data and experimentation on an electric propulsion thruster for small, low-power satellites

- calibrating data analysis from the Stellar X-Ray Polarimeter of the Russian Spectrum Roentgen Gamma spacecraft

- studying the dynamics of the atmospheres of Venus and Mars using multidimensional circulation models, and

- developing an imaging system suitable for use on the Mariner Mark 2 spacecraft and the series of missions proposed for that spacecraft.

In addition, a large number of projects and significant funds have been dedicated to the International Space Station and its related projects.

To examine spending in other fields of science, Figure 3.6 shows spending by fields of science excluding aerospace. This figure shows spending focusing on

RAND*MR1504-3.6*

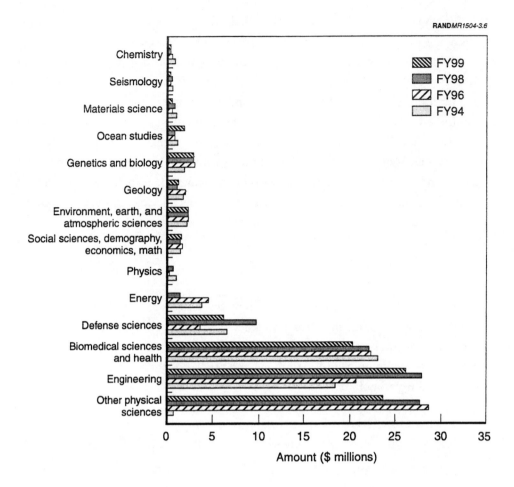

**Figure 3.6—Spending on Areas of S&T Cooperation by Field,
Excluding Aerospace, 1994, 1996, 1998, and 1999**

engineering, energy, biomedical and health sciences, physics, defense sciences, and a collection of projects in the social, demographic, and economic sciences. This breakdown by field has a pattern similar to U.S. cooperation with other scientifically advanced countries—with two exceptions: spending on engineering and on defense sciences is higher with Russia than with other countries. In contrast, spending with Canada and Mexico (again, with the exception of aerospace) is dominated by cooperation in biomedical and earth sciences.

Engineering

Engineering projects include a number of joint research and technical support activities aimed at building capacity in Russia. Spending on average reached $20 million a year; if USAID funds were added,[8] the amount would be considerably higher, perhaps totaling $30 million per year. For example, a project on robotics in construction and environmental restoration operations focused on comparing traditional, human-operated systems with telerobotic and autonomous systems in environmental applications to determine the feasible uses of automated equipment in construction, mining, and environmental cleanups. Another project involved an effort to stabilize the technology infrastructure in Russia and to cultivate technologies that may have future commercial value. Engineering standards development included a project that sought to transfer state-of-the-art reactor system analysis codes to Russia and Ukraine and to support development of internationally accepted analysis standards.

Energy

Energy research activities are dominated by three types of activities: (1) technical support projects to transfer clean and efficient energy technology to Russia, (2) expensive fusion research efforts, and (3) nuclear safety efforts. Projects in energy R&D totaled an average of $20 million a year in the period examined for this study. Examples include

- a project to provide technical assistance and support for energy efficiency and renewable energy activities in support of a joint U.S.–Russia agreement

- an initiative to support the research and development of a lightweight, roof-top boiler system for buildings in Russia, and

- a research project to reduce emissions from fossil fuel power plants located in the former Soviet Union.

Biomedical and Health Sciences

Biomedical and health sciences present perhaps the most diverse set of activities being sponsored with Russia, ranging from infectious disease control to epidemiology to prosthetics. This area of science is also notable because a number of agencies of the U.S. government are involved. Whereas aerospace and energy projects tend to be sponsored by NASA, DOE, and DOD, biomedical and health science projects are sponsored by these three agencies as well as Department of Health and Human Services (HHS) agencies (both NIH and the Centers for Disease Control and Prevention [CDC]), Veterans Affairs, USAID,

---

[8]Recall that USAID funds are not detailed at the project level. However, many projects funded by this agency aim at capacity building in engineering-related activities.

and others. We were able to document totals for biomedical and health sciences R&D averaging $12 million a year. A sample of the range of projects includes

- a comparative analysis of Group A and B streptococcal genome proposal, a collaboration between two participating institutions with a common interest in the study of pathogenic streptococci

- liaison, information sharing, and testing with the National Center for Medical Rehabilitation Research regarding work on lower limb prosthetics

- development of sensitive and specific rapid diagnostic tests for lyme borreliosis in Russia, and

- cooperative efforts to evaluate the factors influencing health risks, the prevalence of sexually transmitted diseases (STDs) and HIV/AIDS, and health-seeking behavior among women in Russia.

Physics

Research in physics has historically been an area where the U.S. government has committed significant amounts to international collaboration, in part because the large-scale equipment needed for many physics experiments is so expensive that nations cooperate to share costs. Physics is often listed among the most active fields for international research. In addition, physics often emerges at the top of the list of scientific fields where international colleagues are co-authoring papers. This may be because scientists meet each other and undertake collaborations at international research centers such as the European Organization for Nuclear Research (CERN). Physics R&D with Russia on both a binational and multinational basis has averaged at least $8.5 million a year since 1994. It was the only area of science to see a significant increase in 1999, in large part because of the initiation of a large multinational physics project in which Russia is a partner: the Compact Muon Solenoid being built at CERN.

Other physics projects being conducted with Russia include

- a cooperative research program on the development of novel theoretical techniques ("nonperturbative expansions") primarily applied to quantum chromodynamics, to advance the theory of strong nuclear interactions

- a joint collaborative effort between American and Russian scientists to develop simple analytic models to describe the dynamic properties of electrons in electric fields, and the dynamic polarizability of Rydberg states, with results applied to experiments using trapped ions, and

- a real-time detector for low-energy solar neutrinos.

How Does U.S. Spending Compare with Russian Priorities?

In an effort to understand how the U.S. government's investment compares with Russian R&D spending, we examined data on Russian federal R&D investment. Table 3.1 compares the U.S. government's investment in the bilateral relationship with Russia's R&D priorities.[9] Based on data reported by the Center for Scientific Research and Statistics in Moscow, U.S. government investment in the bilateral relationship strongly correlates with Russian priorities in four areas: biomedical and health sciences, energy, engineering, and physics. This suggests that U.S. investments in cooperation are finding fertile ground for joint work in these areas.

A common emphasis on defense sciences, environment and earth sciences, ocean studies, and materials sciences also suggests that cooperation in these fields may be productive and useful for both sides. In contrast, U.S. investment in geology, seismology, and social sciences are being made even as Russian R&D funding is relatively weak (even if historical capability is strong), suggesting that perhaps U.S. investment in cooperation in these areas is not being financially matched in any meaningful way.

In contrast, a gap in funding between strong Russian investment in several R&D areas and low U.S. investment in the bilateral relationship suggests that the following areas may be opportunities for enhanced cooperation: chemistry, construction, information technologies, telecommunications, and transportation.

Similar opportunities for joint work may exist in several areas where the Russian government has set aside funds for international cooperation but where the United States is not placing a heavy emphasis. These areas are mining, agricultural genetics, and earth sciences.

Cooperation with Russia by Five U.S. Agencies

Five U.S. government agencies account for 90 percent of the R&D spending on cooperation with Russia: NASA, DOE, HHS (and within HHS, primarily NIH), DOD, and NSF. These agencies are also the largest R&D agencies within the federal government. This section describes the nature of support for cooperation with Russia within these five agencies.

---

[9]Because of the difficulties of determining an annual exchange rate for the Russian ruble prior to 1999 (due to the country's macroeconomic instability), the table uses bullets to indicate heavy, moderate, and light emphasis in investment.

Table 3.1

Comparison of Areas of R&D Emphasis

RAND*MR1504-T3.1*

Field	U.S. government spending on the bilateral relationship	Russian government R&D spending, overall[a]	Russian government R&D spending, international only[b]	Russian S&T excellence measured by publications and citations[c]
Aerospace, astronomy	●	●		◐
Agriculture	○	◐	◐	
Biomedical/health sciences	●	●	●	●
Chemistry		◐		●
Construction		●	○	
Defense sciences	●	◐		
Energy	●	●	◐	
Engineering	●	●	●	◐
Environment and earth sciences	◐	◐	●	◐
Genetics and biology	○	◐	○	◐
Geology	◐			
Information technologies		◐	●	
Materials sciences	◐	●	○	
Mathematics				○
Mining			◐	
Ocean studies	○	◐		
Physics	●	●	●	●
Seismology	○			
Social sciences and economics	○			○
Telecommunications		◐		
Transportation		◐		

● Heavy   ◐ Moderate   ○ Light

[a] Based on 1996 Federal budget appropriations in S&T, reported by the Center for Scientific Research and Statistics.

[b] Based on 1996 budget appropriations for international S&T programs, reported by the Center for Scientific Research and Statistics.

[c] Based on 1995–1997 publications cited in National Science Board, 2000.

National Aeronautics and Space Administration

During the time period examined in this study, NASA ranked first among the mission agencies in the amount of funds it allocated to projects that involve cooperative activities with Russia.

For 1994, 1996, 1998, and 1999, NASA spent an estimated $712.1 million in cooperative activities with Russia to support 143 projects. An annual breakdown shows funding at $171.5 million in 1994, $230.6 million in 1996, $166.1 million in 1998, and $144.0 million in 1999.

The high level of funding in 1996 and 1998 can be attributed to two major activities:

1. The Mars 98 Orbiter and Lander project. In 1996 alone, about $50 million was allocated to R&D of these two instruments. By 1999, much of the R&D was completed and funding shifted to operations support, which required a lower level of funding.

2. Several other large cooperative activities that ended in 1998. They included advanced R&D in aerospace technologies at the Dryden Flight Research Center and data management system work for the International Space Station. Both are bilateral cooperative activities that comprised, on average, about half of all cooperative activities between the United States and Russia in the mid-1990s.

Cooperative activities funded by NASA spanned a number of scientific fields: atomic science, biology, earth sciences, geology, environmental sciences, and oceanography, among others. Nonetheless, the heaviest concentration is in aerospace. The majority of these efforts are joint research projects: 19 out of 25 cooperative activities (or 79 percent) in 1996 and 20 out of 23 cooperative activities (or 86 percent) in 1998; more than half of these collaborative research activities are bilateral efforts.

Examples of joint research include

*   a bilateral project to measure air pollution from Russian space equipment (which ran from 1996 to 1999)

*   a decade-long bilateral project (from 1993 through 2004) under the Joint U.S.-Russian Human Space Flight Activities initiative to conduct applied research and exploratory development activities

*   in 1992, a multilateral cell and developmental biology study began to refine the gravity field of Mars and determine its spin pole orientation, and

- a multilateral study to extend scientific understanding of the interactions between land surface climatology parameters and remote sensing variables to sites in the Eurasian and African continents.

Department of Energy

The Department of Energy commits the second largest amount of federal resources devoted to bilateral and multilateral cooperation with Russia. According to officials at the Office of International Science & Technology Cooperation at DOE, between 1994 and 2000, average annual DOE funding for cooperation with Russia ranged from $200 to $300 million.[10]

Roughly one-third of DOE funding to Russia is devoted to S&T cooperation.[11] Data compiled by RAND for 1994, 1996, 1998, and 1999 show average support of $81 million per year. DOE funding grew to $90.1 million in 1996 and $90.4 million in 1998—an increase of nearly 30 percent from that of 1994. In 1999, funding fell to $71.7 million. During these years, the number of projects conducted with Russia also fluctuated—from 121 projects in 1994 to 133 projects in 1996. The number of projects fell to 106 in 1998 and was further reduced to 58 projects in 1999.[11]

According to its Organic Act, DOE has authority to enter into cooperative S&T agreements with foreign entities, and most of its activities in Russia are pursued at the agency's initiative under this mandate; they are not appropriated separately by Congress.[12] The vast majority of DOE activities and funding in Russia is managed through the Office of Defense Nuclear Nonproliferation and the Office of International Affairs.

According to DOE officials, S&T cooperation with Russia fulfills several DOE objectives:

- To enhance national security, for example, through materials and technologies controls.

---

[10]Personal communication, July 17, 2001. DOE also administers a large number of projects on behalf of other agencies such as USAID and the Department of Defense (e.g., Nunn-Lugar Cooperative Threat Reduction activities). Such projects are not counted in the RAND totals.

[11]The fluctuations in both funding and the number of projects can be attributed to the commencement and conclusion of a few large-scale cooperative ventures that include multiyear funding and multiple project components. One example is the Russian-U.S. Energy Efficiency Work Plan, which, from 1993 through 1998, provided technical assistance and support to a number of energy efficiency and renewable energy activities under the auspices of the Russian-American Memorandum of Cooperation for Energy Efficiency.

[12]DOE does carry out projects for other federal agencies and receives add-on funding to its own initiatives that are the result of specific legislative requirements.

28

- To access facilities and environments not available in the United States, such as locations with high levels of radioactive contamination in which to verify and refine models developed in the United States.

- To utilize unique technologies and capabilities of Russian scientific institutions in areas such as energy engineering, waste management, instrumentation and machine tooling.

- To help develop unique Russian theoretical work and know-how in areas of international significance, such as the tokamak model for fusion science.

- To obtain cost-effective analytical and technical support to U.S.-based S&T ventures.

In most cases, DOE's S&T cooperative activities in Russia are conducted on an institution-to-institution basis, typically involving one or more of DOE's National Laboratories. Given the objectives outlined above, most cooperative work is conducted in Russia, whereas administrative work is handled in the United States. DOE often commits its funding for collaborative research through the ISTC and CRDF, given the favorable tax treatment this contracting mechanism enjoys in Russia. Estimates of Russian contributions to these cooperative efforts have not been made, although DOE officials told us that Russian institutions typically cover local facilities and labor costs.[13] They added that all international travel is fully funded by the sending country.

DOE's cooperative activities between the United States and Russia cut across a range of fields and disciplines and mirror the agency's overall program profile— that is, research activities are focused largely on addressing national security concerns. The top five areas of cooperation are defense (e.g., fissile materials controls and disposition), energy (e.g., civilian nuclear reactor safety), other engineering sciences (e.g., nuclear waste repository engineering), other physical sciences (e.g., high-energy physics), and the environmental sciences (e.g., environmental cleanup and restoration).

Drawing on data gathered by the State Department, Figure 3.7 shows DOE funding by major program for cooperative activities with Russia between 1993 and 2000. (These amounts are higher than we were able to document independently.)

Among the fields outlined above, technical support makes up a large portion of DOE-funded S&T activities with Russia. In fact, of DOE projects conducted with

---

[13]In the fields of nuclear physics and engineering, Russian labor and facility contributions may be more significant, given Russia's relative strength in these areas.

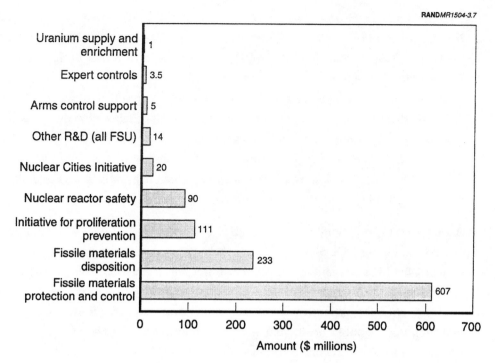

RAND*MR1504-3.7*

SOURCE: U.S. Department of State (2001).

**Figure 3.7—Areas of S&T Research Cooperation in Russia
Funded by DOE, 1993–2000**

Russian scientists, over half are for providing technical support. In 1996, 73 out of 133 projects (55 percent) with Russia entailed technical support; for 1998, the number was 59 of 106 projects (56 percent).

Bilateral technical support includes the Russian-American Energy Efficiency Work Plan and the development of a U.S.-Russia Arctic Oil and Gas Production Guide. The Nuclear Cities Initiative (NCI) seeks to enhance U.S. and global security by restructuring the functions and equipment of the weapons complex and promoting sustainable, nonweapons work to create a diversified city economy. Under NCI, for instance, the Sarov Open Computing Center was opened in 1999 to capitalize on local software engineering talent by generating commercial, nondefense contracts with Russian and international firms.

Multilateral technical support efforts include the Technical Assistance Program for Energy Efficiency in Eastern Europe and the Newly Independent States (NIS) and a nuclear safety program that provided training and equipment for nuclear power stations in the former Soviet Union. Since its inception as a U.S.-Russian program, NCI also has attracted support from multilateral institutions such as the ISTC and the European Bank for Reconstruction and Development.

Joint research is the second most common type of cooperative activity with Russia. For example, collaborative research was involved in 37 of 133 projects (28 percent) in 1996, and in 29 of 106 projects (27 percent) in 1998. The Initiatives for Proliferation Prevention (IPP) program, established in 1994, is an institute-to-institute effort to promote long-term employment opportunities for weapons scientists throughout the former Soviet Union through collaboration on applied research projects having high commercial potential. Through 2000, IPP had funded 102 projects involving scientists, engineers, and technicians working principally in the closed nuclear cities of Sarov, Snezhinsk, and Zheleznogorsk. (IPP is described in more detail in Section 4.)

A smaller number of joint research projects go beyond the national security field and address other DOE S&T interests in areas such as energy engineering, genetics, health, and plant biology. For example, since 1994 DOE has led (with support from the Nuclear Regulatory Commission [NRC], DOD, HHS, and the Environmental Protection Agency [EPA]) a long-term research effort investigating the public health and environmental effects of radiation exposure. The Russian-American Fuel Cell Consortium is a project to develop and commercialize new technologies to support the development of a commercial fuel cell industry. DOE has also funded a study on present and future carbon balance in Russia's northern ecosystems.

Multilateral research efforts include an industrial partnering program to develop a high-power free electron laser for satellite power beaming application and the screening of botanical and fungal species collected in the Newly Independent States. One of DOE's most visible multilateral collaborative research efforts involving Russia in the 1990s was the ITER program, which involved the United States, Russia, Japan, and the European Community.[14]

Department of Health and Human Services

The Department of Health and Human Services cooperates with Russia through the National Institutes of Health, the Office of International and Refugee Health (Office of Europe and the Newly Independent States), and the Centers for Disease Control and Prevention. The total amount spent by HHS agencies on cooperation with Russia averaged about $20 million a year in the 1990s.

The National Institutes of Health, through its research institutes as well as through the John E. Fogarty International Center, has dedicated in the range of

---

[14]In 1999, DOE ended U.S. participation in the ITER program at the request of Congress.

$12 million a year to cooperation with Russia. In 1994 and 1996, R&D projects being conducted cooperatively with Russia (both binational and multinational projects) totaled $12 million per year; R&D spending dropped somewhat in the second half of the 1990s. In 1998, NIH spending on cooperative R&D was $9 million, and in 1999, it dropped again to $7 million. An additional $3 million per year in non-R&D funding was spent by NIH on education and training programs, fellowships, and other joint professional activities with Russia.

The National Cancer Institute was the leading funder of binational cooperative research with Russia, spending on average about $2 million a year on cooperation with Russia during the 1990s. The National Center for Research Resources funded a multinational project, with Russia as one of three partners, at $9 million a year beginning in the early 1990s. Other agencies with investments close to the $500,000 mark were the National Institute on Aging, the National Institute on Child Health and Human Development, and, in 1996, the National Institute on Drug Abuse. Examples of projects funded include

- a Center for Prevention Research within the National Mental Health Research Center of the Russian Academy of Medical Sciences as part of a drug abuse prevention study to provide the mentoring necessary to make the Moscow Center a viable and independent entity
- a look at Russia as part of a comparative study of the health, economic well-being, and behavior of the elderly
- a joint study on radiation resistance of human melanoma cells, and
- an international conference on environmental mutagens with a focus on the pollution problems of the former Soviet Union.

The John E. Fogarty Center sponsored the largest number of joint projects with Russia, about ten per year during the 1990s. The Fogarty Center projects aimed specifically at aiding Russian science. The subjects of the Fogarty Center grants range considerably across fields of science and include genomics, demography, and basic research in chemistry, biology, and physics. The Fogarty Center also sponsored a Visiting Program and the International Research Fellowships, but these activities were phased out in 1999, which may account for part of the drop in funding for that year.

The Office of International and Refugee Health, within the Office for Europe and the NIS, is responsible for administering the Biotechnology Engagement Program (BTEP). BTEP was developed as part of the U.S. government's effort to combat proliferation of weapons of mass destruction as well as to reduce the threat of bioterrorism. The program aims to engage former Soviet biological weapons scientists in projects of collaborative research focusing on pubic health problems. Although HHS is a partner in these activities with the International Science and Technology Center (a special project described in more detail below), HHS puts very little funding into this activity. BTEP is primarily funded by a congressional appropriation administered by the Department of State.

Research conducted through BTEP includes rapid diagnosis of strains of tuberculosis and hepatitis, as well as West Nile encephalitis. Other work focuses on HIV/AIDS and infectious diseases such as measles and mumps, and includes epidemiology training for scientist and technicians. At least 70 percent of the funding under this program is transferred to researchers in the Newly Independent States.

The Centers for Disease Control and Prevention is working actively in Russia on a range of projects, some of which are funded by the Cooperative Threat Reduction program, some funded by USAID, and a few funded by CDC itself. (Some of these projects go beyond the scope of S&T activities covered in this report.) The list below provides an sampling of CDC activities with Russia, derived from CDC's *Global Health Activities Annual Report, Fiscal Year 1998.*

- Birth Defects/Neonatal Screening: As part of an international quality-assurance program, CDC provided performance evaluation materials for Russia's two neonatal screening laboratories.

- Cardiovascular Disease: CDC collaborated on a project to increase the effectiveness of cardiovascular disease prevention in Russia.

- Cholesterol and Related Lipids—Laboratory Standardization: CDC worked with lipid research labs in Russia to test and standardize laboratory diagnostic methods.

- HIV/AIDS: As part of a collaborative study, CDC worked with Russian counterparts to evaluate the factors influencing health risks and the prevalence of disease in high-risk subgroups within the Russian population.

National Science Foundation

NSF funding for cooperative R&D activities with Russia remained steady between 1994 and 1998, with a slight increase in 1999. In 1994, the number of activities funded was 268; that number decreased to 148 by 1999 (Figure 3.8). Although the *number of projects* reached its lowest point by 1999, the *funding* increased to its highest point of $21.6 million in that year. The funding for bilateral activities averaged $6.6 million a year between 1994 and 1999. In

RAND*MR1504-3.8*

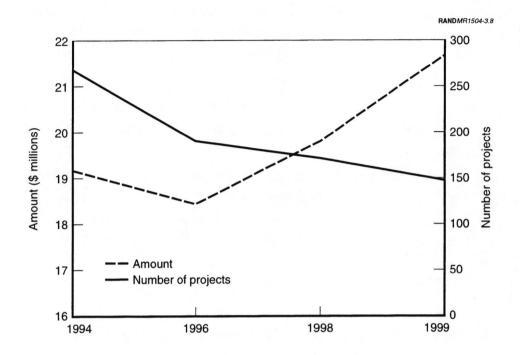

Figure 3.8—NSF Funding for Cooperative Activities with Russia

comparison, NSF funding for bilateral activities with Mexico grew from $2 million in 1993 to $4.5 million in 1997; and with Canada, from $1.9 million to $6 million in those same years. Funding for multilateral activities involving Russia averaged $12.5 million a year between 1994 and 1998 and increased to $14.5 million in 1999.

Of the various government agencies, NSF funds the largest number of projects with Russia across the broadest range of scientific fields. Fields represented (in order of number of projects) are earth sciences—which encompass geology, seismology, oceanography, and atmospheric sciences—and the physical sciences—chemistry, physics, and materials science.

In addition, NSF is one of only a few U.S. government agencies to fund projects in the social sciences (e.g., demography, economics, sociology, anthropology). Within the NSF's organizational structure, the leading directorates funding science with Russia are, in descending order, the Directorate for Social, Behavioral, and Economic Sciences (housing the Division of International Programs where a number of projects with Russia are funded); Geosciences; and U.S. Polar Research Programs.

On average, 75 percent of the NSF-funded activities with Russia are collaborative projects, followed by 15 percent of spending to support conferences. Examples of bilateral collaborative projects include

- a comparative study of the lives of women and children in two Yupik Eskimo communities in Alaska and Russia, who both identify themselves as Yupik but have experienced very different histories due to Western policies and cultures

- deciphering the record of Quaternary glaciations on Novaya Zemlya, Russia to develop boundaries for evolving global climate models, and

- an investigation to examine Arctic Ocean temperature and to relate fluctuations to changes in atmospheric forcing in surrounding regions.

Examples of multilateral collaborative projects include

- collaboration with and among U.S., Russian, and Japanese scientists to study the Okhotsk Sea and East Sakhalin Current for measurements of water properties and hydrographic surveys

- collaboration with and among U.S., Russian, Japanese, and Vietnamese scientists to study and understand the origin of cosmic rays, and

- collaboration among U.S., Russian, Ukrainian, and Lithuanian scientists to study the growing controversy regarding the formation of political parties and party systems in post-Soviet societies.

In 1997, the U.S.-Russian Binational (formerly Gore-Chernomyrdin) Commission's Science and Technology Committee initiated four S&T agreements between NSF and Russian research institutions:

- A memorandum of understanding (MOU) with the Russian Ministry for Science and Technologies for cooperation in high-performance scientific computing. Scientists have been cooperating on networking, digital libraries, and developing new research agendas.

- Incorporated Research Institutions for Seismology (funded by NSF/Geosciences), the U.S. Geological Survey, and the Russian Academy of Sciences are cooperating in improving both new data-exchange methods and the seismological network in Russia, to ensure better seismic safety and monitoring of global nuclear explosions.

- NSF signed an MOU with its Russian counterpart, the Russian Foundation for Basic Research (RFBR), to cooperate in Arctic climatology and ecology and to support young investigators. Through the agreement, NSF and RFBR have also developed new math initiatives and a project with the National Institutes of Health regarding infectious diseases.

• The Baikal Drilling Project is a multinational agreement involving NSF/Geosciences, the Institute of Geochemistry of the Siberian Branch of the Russian Academy of Sciences, and institutions in Germany and Japan. The collaboration involves drilling ice cores from Lake Baikal to develop a record of climate and environmental change in Eurasia over the last 10 million years.

NSF is involved in many other types of multilateral agreements in which Russia is a partner. One such project is FLYBRAIN, a federation of interactive insect neuroanatomy databases with Germany, Japan, and Russia. Another example is the NSF/Geosciences National Center for Atmospheric Research, which collaborates with atmospheric research institutions in Canada, Germany, Australia, and Russia.

NSF supports international research centers in the United States that are open to visiting scientists and students from other countries. For example, the National High Magnetic Field Laboratory[15] is involved in international cooperation initiated by the Los Alamos National Laboratory and the All-Russian Institute of Experimental Physics. Scientists from the United States, Russia, Britain, and Japan are collaborating to provide extremely high magnetic fields utilizing explosive-driven flux compression techniques.

NSF also supports several Science and Technology Centers to promote long-term multi- and interdisciplinary collaborative research, much of which includes an international component. For example, scientists from Michigan State University Center for Microbial Ecology and the Russian Academy of Science collaborate with each other in studies of microorganisms in permafrost soil cores and microbial carbon cycle in the Siberian wetlands.[16]

In 1995, NSF played a role in establishing the U.S. Civilian Research and Development Foundation (CRDF) for the Independent States of the former Soviet Union under a congressional authorization. Between 1995 and 2000, the U.S. government, through NSF, gave $49.9 million to CRDF for its programs.[17] Of this funding, $12.5 million was directly from NSF.

---

[15]The National High Magnetic Field Laboratory is funded by NSF and operated by Florida State University, Los Alamos National Laboratory, and the University of Florida.

[16]Many of the foregoing examples are from National Science Foundation (1998).

[17]Fiscal year accounting does not perfectly match the level of CRDF activities in Russia. While monies awarded to collaboration by NSF and other government agencies are likely to have been spent in the fiscal year noted, monies allocated to CRDF and ISTC (see below) allocated in one fiscal

Department of Defense

DOD cooperation with Russia is substantial, but the share of these activities paid for out of R&D budgets is relatively small. DOD does not provide budget data that would allow a full picture of its activities; however, we estimate that DOD's R&D spending with Russia dropped from about $5 million in 1994 to about $2 million in 1999. This amount includes projects sponsored by the Ballistic Missile Defense Organization; the Departments of the Air Force, Navy, and Army; and the Office of the Secretary of Defense. In addition, funds from DOD transferred to other agencies supported as much as $2 million per year in activities related to aerospace and atmospheric science.

Oceanography and atmospheric sciences account for the largest number of projects funded by DOD. These include projects sponsored by the Navy in acoustic tomography, ocean circulation, the relationship between the oceans and the atmosphere, and a number of studies focusing on many aspects of the Arctic Ocean. Aerospace-related projects, funded through the Navy, Air Force, and as transfers to NASA, cover a broad range: from studying space sensors and other remote sensing tools; electric propulsion for small, low-power satellites; and solar radar experiments; to the development of visible and infrared mapping spectrometers; tests of relativistic gravity; and other basic scientific studies.

Over and above the R&D activities, DOD funds a number of projects with Russia that have a scientific or technical component. Many of these projects are funded through the Cooperative Threat Reduction program and are aimed at national security goals specific to Russia. These include such projects as contributions to the Collaborative Biotechnology Programs, the Defense Enterprise Fund, and the Defense Conversion Fund. The cumulative amounts devoted to these activities total in the hundreds of millions of dollars each year—these funds are not accounted for in this report. These technical activities aimed at specific national security goals include projects such as

- weapons destruction and dismantlement

- "chain of custody" projects healing to prevent the proliferation of nuclear materials

- demilitarization and defense conversion (including efforts to commercialize technologies coming out of the defense labs and the Defense Enterprise Fund to help commercial entities), and

---

year are not likely to be distributed to researchers for another one to two years because of a more extended project review period.

- a collaborative biotechnology program to fund collaborative biotechnical research with former bioweapons scientists.

4. The Mission-Oriented and Policy-Directed S&T Relationships with Russia

Between 1994 and 1999, U.S. government spending on cooperative mission-oriented and policy-directed S&T activities averaged $56 million per year. This figure is an estimate based on reporting by federal government agencies. (The RaDiUS database does not contain information on S&T activities that are not classified by federal agencies as "research and development." See Appendix 2.) Federal government agency officials view the activities reported in this section as part of the overall S&T relationship with Russia. Many of these activities derive from specific agency missions. In some cases, the U.S. agency has been directed by Congress to undertake these activities with Russia.

Within the $56 million a year of spending on projects with Russia, the following types of activities are included:

- non-R&D projects within three agencies described in Section 3: DOD, DOE, and HHS

- activities of a number of smaller agencies of government—ones that do not have large R&D budgets—in their support projects with Russia

- activities funded by federal agencies that support the special programs described at the end of this section as policy-directed S&T activities.

Unlike the many curiosity-driven R&D projects described in Section 3, the agencies described in this section generally fund activities with Russia to help meet mission-specific requirements. The agencies discussed in this section are the U.S. Agency for International Development (USAID), the U.S. Department of Agriculture (USDA), the Department of State, the Federal Emergency Management Agency (FEMA), the Department of Commerce's National Institute for Standards and Technology, and the Department of Interior's U.S. Geological Survey (USGS).

U.S. Agency for International Development

Promoting democratic and market reforms are the main thrusts of USAID activities with Russia. USAID also funds humanitarian activities to support social transition, particularly in promoting sustainable social services and health, an area where USAID works with a number of U.S., Russian, and international organizations.

USAID's assistance and economic cooperation strategy for Russia is part of a broader strategy that encompasses all of the Newly Independent States of the former Soviet Union (USAID, 1995).

The Freedom Support Act (FSA) assistance to Russia is a major source of USAID funds for activities with Russia. In 2000, USAID programs accounted for approximately $61 million of the $168 million allocated under FSA for Russia.[1] A breakdown of USAID activities supported by FSA assistance includes

- $16 million for private-sector development and economic restructuring
- $14 million for democratic reform
- $11 million for health
- $4 million for environmental programs
- $3 million for urban socioeconomic programs
- $3 million for exchanges, training, and special initiatives
- $7 million for the Eurasia Foundation.

The Bureau for Europe and Eurasia manages activities with Russia. In the period immediately following the collapse of the Soviet Union, humanitarian aid was the primary focus. In the second phase, attention shifted to technical assistance, training, and exchanges directed at helping Russia to create laws, regulations, and institutions necessary for a democracy and market economy to function. A third phase was to commence in 1998 when all new technical assistance obligations to Russia would cease and emphasis would shift to increasing direct support for trade and investment to spur private-sector development in Russia.

However, devaluation of the ruble in 1998 fundamentally altered economic, social, and political conditions in Russia. As a result, USAID modified its program approach to emphasize partnerships with civil society and interventions at the regional level. Technical assistance focused on training and other activities to promote market reforms in banking, finance, energy, and other sectors (USAID, 2001a). Approximately 9,000 Russian professionals have participated in USAID-funded short-term training program in the United States, Russia, and other countries since 1993 (U.S. Department of State, 2001). These include

---

[1]In 2000, FSA assistance to Russia, as in previous years, was subjected to a 50 percent cut mandated by the U.S. Congress as a punitive measure for alleged Russian transfers of nuclear technology to Iran.

- the Global Training Program for Development, which supports more than 2,000 Russian participants in 80 training programs. The Global Training Program was launched in 1997 and implemented by the Academy for Educational Development. However, support for Russia has declined sharply since 2000 with a shift of emphasis to the Caucasus and Central Asia (U.S. Department of State, 2001, pp. 179–183)

- the Eurasia Foundation, which was established in 1993 with major funding from USAID, to promote democratic and market economic reforms at the grassroots level in the 12 NIS countries (U.S. Department of State, 2001, p. 300), and

- a training program to promote and adopt international accounting standards in Russia.

Environmental programs focus mainly on the energy and forestry sectors. Activities in the energy sector emphasize training and reforms to increase energy efficiency and promote sustainable energy use. Activities in the forestry sector emphasize reforestation and improvements in forestry policy and forest fire management.[2]

In the health sector, USAID has, since 1992, provided over $120 million and trained more than 10,000 Russian health professionals to address health issues and strengthen Russia's health system. USAID implements its health program in cooperation with the Russian Ministry of Health and health officials and medical service providers at all levels of the Russian government. USAID also collaborated with the U.S. Centers for Disease Control and Prevention, the National Institutes of Health, the World Health Organization (WHO), and various nonprofit and private-sector organizations supported by USAID (U.S. Department of State, 2001; USAID, 2001a).

Priorities in USAID's health program with Russia were established by the U.S.-Russian Health Committee, formed in 1994 under the U.S.-Russia Binational Commission. The five key areas of current USAID collaboration in health and major activities are the following:

- women and infant health: training health practitioners, strengthening counseling skills, and developing family planning guidelines

- HIV/AIDS/STD prevention: HIV prevention among high-risk groups, training health workers, and laboratory equipment upgrades

---

[2]USAID, *USAID Climate Change Initiative 1998–2002*, at http://www.usaid.gov/environment/pubs/cci_usaidgec.pdf.

- tuberculosis treatment and control: adapting and introducing to Russia the diagnosis and treatment approach developed by WHO

- health care quality and reform: improving prevention and treatment practices in the Russian health system and developing care and clinical guidelines, and

- health partnerships: 22 partnerships (15 completed) to promote more effective and efficient delivery of community-based, primary health care (USAID, 2001b).

Department of Agriculture

Between 1992 and 2000, according to USDA officials, that agency spent a total of $10 million in assistance programs with Russia. This was about one-fifth of the total funding, or $51 million, for assistance programs with the NIS during this period. This ranks Russia second behind Armenia, which received $27.9 million in the same period.[3] In contrast, activities with Russia included fellowships, faculty exchange, and collaborative research. Moreover, funding for activities with Russia surpassed funding for activities with the other NIS in all categories except faculty exchange in Ukraine.

USDA S&T cooperation with Russia has focused primarily on training, technical support, and collaborative research. Major USDA assistance programs with Russia are the Cochran Fellowship Program, the Faculty Exchange Program, and the Collaborative Research Program. The USDA Foreign Agriculture Service (USDA/FAS) manages the first two and the USDA Agricultural Research Service (USDA/ARS) manages the third.

The Cochran Fellowship Program provides short-term agricultural training for NIS agriculturalists and policymakers. Training programs are conducted in the United States for selected mid- and senior-level specialists and administrators to help improve the agricultural food system in the NIS and to strengthen their agricultural trade links with U.S. agribusiness. In 2000, there were 35 fellows from Russia. The Cochran Fellowship Program also received funds from the Emerging Markets Program of USDA/FAS for training in wholesale and retail marketing. In 2000, USDA reported that 14 Cochran Fellows funded by the Emerging Markets Office of USDA/FAS came to the United States from Russia, Ukraine, and Uzbekistan.

---

[3]It is important to point out that of the sum received by Armenia, $27.15 million went to the Armenia Marketing Assistance Program and $750,000 to fellowships.

42

The Faculty Exchange Program provides six months of practical training to university educators from progressive NIS agricultural institutions to increase their capacity to develop academic and adult education programs and curricula in agricultural economics and marketing, agribusiness, and agrarian law. Collaborative research has not been a component of this program, but recently the University of Nebraska at Lincoln and the Moscow State Agro-Engineering University began exploring the possibility of establishing joint research programs. Also, Colorado State University researchers and past program participants from Russia have proposed joint research activities on vertical integration of agriculture in the Orel and Voronezh regions of Russia, risk management in agriculture, and other topics. Funding proposals for some of this research were submitted to the USDA/National Research Initiative Competitive Grants Program in early 2001.

The Department of State (Office of Proliferation Threat Reduction and Office of the U.S. Coordinator) funds the USDA/ARS Collaborative Research Program for NIS Assistance. USDA/ARS staff told us that, given the limited resources for international research activities within USDA/ARS, this effort allows USDA/ARS to leverage resources from other U.S. mission agencies. Projects in Russia are implemented through the International Science and Technology Center in Moscow. Participating institutes include the All-Russian Research Institute for Animal Health in Vladimir, the State Research Center for Applied Microbiology in Obolensk, and the State Research Center for Virology and Biotechnology in Koltsovo. Seven projects are under way with Russia and seven more have been approved for funding, for a total of $4.7 million. Animal and plant health is the main focus of these studies. Examples are projects to develop a new live vaccine against swine fever and protein engineering of Bacillus thuringiensis insecticidal proteins.

USDA/ARS has also collaborated with the Vavilov Institute in St. Petersburg to jointly develop a germplasm samples collection. The ARS considers the Vavilov Institute's extensive plant germplasm collection to be very important and has committed resources to its long-term preservation. Another USDA/ARS effort is with the Russian Academy of Sciences—Far Eastern Branch in Vladivostok to evaluate Russian honeybees for their resistance to a type of external parasitic mites. U.S. researchers believe that findings might benefit a U.S. breeding program to improve an existing stock of mite-resistant honeybees.

In all these research collaborations, Russia has provided in-kind contributions, including salaries for Russian scientists, travel support to the United States for training, land for agricultural experiments, equipment, and intellectual input to the studies.

USDA/ARS officials reported that cooperation with Russia increases U.S. knowledge about agricultural conditions in Russia, including plant species and animal diseases that are absent in the United States. Such information can help to improve U.S. agricultural research and protect U.S. agriculture—for instance, against foreign invasive species.

In addition to the above projects, the USDA National Agricultural Statistics Services (USDA/NASS) has been active in S&T related activities with Russia. USDA/NASS, which is responsible for gathering and disseminating agricultural statistics in the United States, has been working with the State Committee on Statistics in Russia since 1996 to improve Russian capacity in statistical data collection and dissemination. For example, NASS staff trained their Russian counterparts in conducting sample surveys of farmers and private households, something never done before in Russia. The Emerging Markets Program has funded these activities with Russia at the level of about $150,000 per year. This money goes primarily to reimburse NASS for staff salaries and travel expenses to Russia (seminars are conducted mainly in Russia); and a small fraction goes to travel support for Russians who come to train in the United States. The Russian government has contributed to this effort by paying for staff time, the cost of data collection, and the publication of statistical data in Russian and English. USDA staff reported that this activity has a fairly high level of support in Russia and observed that improved Russian agricultural statistics benefit U.S. agricultural researchers and exporters.

The USDA Economic Research Service (USDA/ERS) also conducted statistical training in Russia that was paid for by the Emerging Markets Office. Apart from this technical support activity, USDA/ERS allocated $10,000 of its own funds in 1995–1996 in a cooperative agreement with the Russian Institute for the Economy in Transition. The agreement's research goal was to compute for the first time producer subsidy equivalents for Russia. This successful collaboration produced data for USDA/ERS and a journal article that has been widely cited.

Department of State

The Department of State has broad overview responsibilities for the S&T relationship with Russia. In addition to helping coordinate the international S&T agreements between the United States and Russia, State provides funding for and helps to oversee the operations of three special programs related to S&T: the International Science and Technology Center, the Civilian Research and Development Foundation, and the Biotechnology Engagement Program. Each of these programs is described elsewhere in this report because they are primarily administered outside of the State Department. The ISTC and CRDF are described in the section on Policy-Directed S&T programs, below, and the BTEP program is described in the subsection on the Department of Health and Human Services in Section 3.

Overall, State has been the agency responsible for passing funds to these activities. The authority to do this was provided to State through the Freedom Support Act and the Cooperative Threat Reduction Act. An average of $15 million per year has been provided to State to support the S&T relationship with Russia since 1992.

Other Agencies

The interests of the U.S. government in a relationship with Russia extend beyond the missions of the R&D agencies. In addition to the ones above, other agencies of government have established or strengthened ties with Russian counterparts.

Federal Emergency Management Agency

The Federal Emergency Management Agency, an independent agency of the federal government, has sponsored technical exchanges with the Russian government in areas such as radiological emergency preparedness, flood management, and search and rescue. A major effort has been a joint real-time simulation on catastrophic disaster in Russia in which both sides shared preparedness and management techniques. U.S. government resources committed to these activities totaled about $1 million a year; most of the funds were transferred to FEMA from USAID. The U.S. government gained know-how by viewing the excellent Russian disaster preparedness techniques, according to FEMA officials.

Environmental Protection Agency

The Environmental Protection Agency carries out a broad range of environmental activities with Russian counterparts, including some collaborative research. During the latter part of the 1990s, EPA received about $1 million a year in appropriations under the Freedom Support Act to support environmental cooperation with Russia. Much of the effort has been directed at supporting Russian implementation of international environmental regimes such as the Montreal Protocol, the London Convention, and the United Nations Environmental Program convention on persistent organic pollutants. Projects often focus on inventory and assessment of pollutant sources, planning for reduction programs, and aid to remediation efforts. The projects usually involve substantial multinational financing.

National Institute for Standards and Technology

The National Institute for Standards and Technology, a laboratory within the Department of Commerce, has maintained a relationship with counterparts that began prior to the breakup of the Soviet Union. The relationship involves consultations about metrology to ensure comparability of measures across a range of scientific and technical areas. Cooperative activities have included measures in time and frequency, mass, and pressure. No additional funds are allocated to work specifically with Russia—consultations are conducted in the course of the agency's mission-related activities.

U.S. Geological Survey

U.S. Geological Survey cooperative activities with Russia peaked in the late 1990s. From 1991 through 1998, funding for U.S.-Russian projects was approximately $9.5 million, with a majority of the funds from the National Science Foundation and USAID. In 1999 and 2000, the level of cooperative activity with Russia fell substantially, with annual expenditures estimated at less than $300,000. The majority of these funds were devoted to travel and salary costs for USGS employees to have scientist-to-scientist contact for data exchange or for relatively small projects.

Since the breakup of the Soviet Union, USGS project activity in Russia has gradually shifted away from basic research in favor of more applied science. This shift reflects greater Russian willingness to share data on energy and mineral resources as well as an increased emphasis on applied geoscience research by U.S. government agencies.

From 1994 to 1998, the USGS (with USAID funding) provided technical assistance to the Russian Ministry of Natural Resources in the field of petroleum geology. Another major program during this period (funded by the State Department) was the creation of an environmental geographic information system of the Selenga River and delta, Lake Baikal Region. The USGS cooperated with the Russian Federal Service for Geodesy and Cartography, the Russian Ministry of Natural Resources, and regional environmental committees in the Lake Baikal area (USGS, 1998). Most recently, USGS activities with Russia are occurring under an MOU (valid until 2004) with the Ministry of Natural

Resources and the Russian Academy of Sciences. One main area of cooperation has been in energy and mineral resources. For example, the USGS is cooperating with the Vernadsky State Geological Museum to develop data sets about gas and oil pipelines. A second main area of cooperation concerns natural hazards—for instance, characterizing seismic properties in the upper crust and mantle, resulting in the acquisition of Russian seismological data. Another project is monitoring 29 potentially active volcanoes on the Kamchatka Peninsula of Russia and 30 active volcanoes in the Kurile Island chain to the south (USGS, 2001).

The Policy-Directed S&T Relationship with Russia (Special Projects)

In contrast to the R&D relationship between the U.S. and Russia—which builds on Russia's scientific excellence—and the mission-oriented S&T support relationship, there are several special programs designed to aid Russia. This aid focuses both on enhancing a peaceful scientific infrastructure in Russia and on using science to solve specific problems (such as the spread of disease) or meet other U.S. goals (such as collecting atmospheric data). A variety of programs and initiatives in the U.S.–Russia S&T relationship have been developed to address a range of policy interests, most notably nonproliferation of weapons of mass destruction. This section describes the U.S. government's role in several of these special projects.

The Civilian Research and Development Foundation

The U.S. Civilian Research and Development Foundation was established in August 1995 by the National Science Foundation, an agency of the federal government, with an initial grant of $5 million appropriated for that purpose through the Cooperative Threat Reduction Act. CRDF is a nonprofit charitable organization created by Congress in 1995, pursuant to Section 511 of the Freedom Support Act of 1992. Its mission is to conduct innovative activities of mutual benefit that help sustain the civilian scientific and technical capability of the countries of the former Soviet Union (FSU). The National Science Foundation and the Department of State share oversight of the U.S. government's interest in CRDF.

Since its inception, CRDF has committed over $29 million of U.S. government funds, or about $6 million a year. The program has managed over $40 million worth of investments, with major contracts from DOE, DOD, NIH, and EPA, as well as industry. Over $10 million has been contributed to CRDF from private foundations. The countries of the former Soviet Union have also committed $5 million to these activities. CRDF funds have supported a total of over 600 projects supporting more than 4,500 scientists and engineers, including over 1,000 young scientists. More than 50 percent of the share of this total has gone to cooperation with Russia.

CRDF operates by providing funding through a competitive grant program. Through a variety of scheduled or ongoing competitions, CRDF selects awards for cooperative projects between the United States and countries of the FSU in basic, applied, and industry-oriented sciences. Through these programs, CRDF grantees receive individual financial support, purchase equipment and supplies, and travel to scientific meetings.

A primary focus of CRDF is to offer opportunities for former weapons scientists to transition to productive civilian research. A total of 250 projects costing roughly $12 million have engaged over 800 defense scientists in civilian projects, primarily within civilian R&D groups.

Another goal of CRDF is to help move applied research to the marketplace and bring economic benefits both to the countries of the FSU and to the United States. CRDF works with U.S. private industry to reduce the risks and costs of initiating industrial R&D collaborations with the countries of the FSU. The CRDF grants have leveraged $4 million in cash and in-kind contributions from U.S. industry. Specifically, the Next Steps to Market program provides grants for pre-commercial, cooperative R&D Projects that are carried out by a team of U.S. and Russian scientists and engineers. The CRDF investment in each project typically averages $75,000 for a period of up to two years.

CRDF is helping to prevent the dissolution of the scientific and technological infrastructure of the FSU by building new, sustainable institutions that promote transition to the market economy and democratization. CRDF's collaborative grants program and scientific institute-building activities teach FSU scientists to compete in the international system of competitive funding. Over 500 research grants and more than 20 center-based activities reach all countries of the FSU. Specifically, the Basic Research and Higher Education program, funded with private grants from the John D. MacArthur Foundation and the Carnegie Corporation of New York, seeks to improve the higher education infrastructure for scientific research by establishing Research and Education Centers within Russian universities. The Regional Experimental Support Center program provides major state-of-the-art equipment and training to selected applied research centers in the FSU, as a shared regional resource for nonprofit educational and industrial research.

Finally, through its Grant Assistance Program, CRDF is helping the U.S. government and industry address issues of financial integrity in the FSU.

The Initiatives for Proliferation Prevention Program

The Initiatives for Proliferation Prevention program was established in 1994 to stabilize defense institutes in the FSU and promote long-term employment opportunities for weapons scientists. IPP, administered by DOE, achieves nonproliferation objectives by engaging scientists, engineers, and technicians from the FSU—primarily Russia, Ukraine, Belarus and Kazakhstan—to develop commercially viable nonweapons projects. This redirection of activities toward peaceful applications is intended to lead to commercial benefits for both the FSU and the United States. Through a unique cost-sharing process, IPP supports FSU–U.S. partnerships that reduce the risk of doing business in the FSU and seek to create successful commercial enterprises. U.S. government funding through 1998 totaled $114 million contributed through the DOE budget.

Sixty thousand former Soviet weapons scientists, engineers, and technicians have been subject to sharp government funding cutbacks at their research institutes since the demise of the Soviet Union. An estimated 90 percent or more of these key professionals are in Russia. Since program inception in 1994, IPP—working institute-by-institute and scientist-by-scientist—has engaged over 10,000 FSU scientists, engineers, and technicians: 5,000 are engaged in currently active projects (an increase of almost 2,000 from 1999).

While several other U.S. government initiatives are also aimed at preventing weapons of mass destruction proliferation, IPP has a unique approach. It seeks to create a phased process to move beyond cooperative research and development to eventually form commercial partnerships between U.S. industry and the former Soviet facilities. Two entities are used to pursue commercialization:

- the Inter-Laboratory Board, made up of members from ten of the DOE National Laboratories, plus the Kansas City Plant, initiates contacts with FSU institutes and performs capabilities evaluations and technology assessments

- the United States Industry Coalition, made up of participating U.S. companies, evaluates commercial potential of the proposed projects, promoting those that have the potential to be implemented cost-effectively, that are attractive to investors, and that may be commercially viable.

Among the specific accomplishments noted by IPP in its literature:

- the program has funded over 400 projects at 170 institutes, including 132 U.S. industry cost-shared projects

- industry has contributed $101 million to these projects, leveraging DOE's investment, and

- in 2000, 194 projects were under way at 88 institutes in Russia, Ukraine, and Kazakhstan.

In total, IPP has funded 102 projects in the closed nuclear cities of Russia, principally Sarov, Snezhinsk, and Zheleznogorsk.

The International Science and Technology Center

The International Science and Technology Center was established by international agreement between the European Union, Japan, the Russian Federation, and the United States in November 1992. It is a nonproliferation program designed to provide peaceful research opportunities to weapons scientists and engineers in the former Soviet Union. The Center expanded its capabilities throughout the 1990s, coordinating the efforts and resources of numerous member governments, public and international organizations, and private industry. Many ISTC programs and activities support other nonproliferation initiatives. The Department of State represents the U.S. government at ISTC meetings.

The objectives of the ISTC are to

- provide weapons scientists in the FSU the opportunity to redirect their talents to peaceful activities

- support basic and applied research and technology development

- contribute to the transition to market-based economies, and

- foster the integration of scientists and engineers from FSU states into the global scientific community.

The ISTC, which began operations at its Moscow headquarters in 1994, continues to play a central role in U.S. government nonproliferation programs. This includes coordinating the resources and talents of numerous governments, national and international laboratories, and public and private-sector organizations to provide FSU weapons scientists with material and logistic support for their peaceful research projects. ISTC activities and programs encourage the integration of FSU scientists into the international community.

Of the $61.8 million of grants issued by the ISTC, the U.S. government contributed an average of $16 million a year during the 1990s. The Department of State estimates that, of this total, about $9 million a year went to fund projects with or in Russia. The grant funds from the ISTC have supported a total of 237 projects among all FSU countries through the Science Project Program, and 76 projects through the Partner Program. Areas of science where grant proposals were slated to receive special attention in the 2000 round included environmental monitoring and remediation, biotechnology research, disposal and safeguarding of nuclear materials, and efficient power production.

The ISTC has given direct grant payments to more than 21,000 scientists and their team members at 400 FSU institutes in 2000, amounting to $26.8 million. In addition, the ISTC has provided business management training courses for 280 project participants in seven cities throughout the FSU. Funding for travel has supported 1,590 scientific team members to participate in conferences and technical meetings.

In November 2000, the ISTC members participated in a review of their activities, resulting in a publication entitled *Year 2000 Review of the ISTC*. ISTC members confirmed their continuing commitment to the Center's goals and objectives. The members note that the ISTC is now a mature organization and an effective platform from which solutions to national and international technical problems can be explored and organized.

ISTC projects for all FSU countries are shown in Table 4.1 by field of science and by order of total funding.

Table 4.1

ISTC Funding by Field of Science

Field of Science	Cumulative Funding from All Sources, 1994-2000, $ million (# of projects)
Environmental sciences	$61 (197)
Biotechnology and life sciences	$50 (208)
Fission reactors	$43 (133)
Physics	$42 (185)
Materials	$35 (107)
Space, aircraft, and surface transportation	$17 (59)
Chemistry	$12 (49)
Information and communications	$11 (49)
Fusion	$9 (31)
Non-nuclear energy	$6 (24)
Manufacturing technology	$4 (26)
Other basic sciences	$3 (14)
Other types of research	$0.5 (7)

5. Observations on the Relationship: Results of Conversations with Scientists and Managers

Data on spending provide useful insights and helpful indicators into the U.S.-Russia S&T relationship. However, to provide more detail, we conducted conversations with 35 U.S.-funded scientists based in the United States and project managers who have participated in or facilitated collaborations with Russian counterparts. While not a formal survey (we could not take statistical account of bias, for example), these conversations added a richness and texture to our understanding of the bilateral relationship. These conversations also were conducted to help us better understand how the relationship is working and to get a sense of the extent to which Russia is matching or otherwise contributing to this research.

Using RaDiUS, we identified a total of 130 bilateral and multilateral collaborative research projects covering a range of scientific disciplines (excluding aerospace-related activities) and their principal investigators. Investigators were contacted by telephone and asked to comment on seven questions as they related to their experience in the project identified. (The discussion protocol is presented in Appendix D.)

The following principal observations emerged from these conversations with U.S. scientists and project managers:

- In more than half of the projects discussed, the Russian collaborators were making at least an equal contribution to the effort.

- The Russian contribution was generally in the form of in-kind support rather than matching funds.

- Assistance was particularly important in helping U.S. researchers obtain documentation and other official approval for research-related activities.

- In three-quarters of the projects discussed, research took place exclusively or largely in Russia.

- Research conducted in Russia focused heavily on data collection.

- Overwhelmingly, discussants reported that the research in question could not have taken place without Russian collaboration.

- The majority of discussants said that the United States benefited, usually in quite significant ways, from this research.

- More than half of the discussants reported that the collaborative research efforts in which they were involved either helped to preserve or build scientific or technical capacity in Russia.

The general impression one gets from these conversations is the broad range of scientific inquiry being pursued. The representatives with whom we spoke were involved in research largely in six areas: the earth sciences (e.g., oceanography, geology, geography), engineering, energy, math, economics, and biology.[1] Twenty of the projects have resulted in papers published in peer-reviewed journals—many of them co-authored with Russian counterparts—or papers that were in the process of being written. In nine of the projects, valuable new databases were created. Among the project representatives with whom we spoke, most were still actively involved with their Russian counterparts: Many projects were still in progress or plans were in place for follow-on work. Researchers on only one project reported that it had failed to achieve the goals it set out to accomplish.

Observations

Type of Collaboration

The majority of researchers reported that the research in question was collaborative in nature—the scientists were working with their counterparts in Russia toward a common scientific goal. Six of the researchers said that the cooperative activities consisted primarily of offering technical support to Russian activities. Five respondents said that the creation of a database was the main reason for the cooperation with Russia.

A number of researchers chose more than one type of collaboration as characterizing their projects with Russia. While the RAND team adhered to the rule of assigning each project (from the list derived from the RaDiUS database) to just one type of cooperative category (see Appendix B), the researchers with whom we spoke were not similarly restricted. Given this flexibility, several added that, in addition to their joint research, the project also offered technical support to Russian scientists, created databases, or was helping to set international research standards.

---

[1]We chose not to contact researchers working on defense-related topics.

54

Location of Research

Three-quarters of the scientists reported that their projects took place primarily in Russia. Most of these were field visits to Russia to collect samples or to access data at Russian institutions. In most cases, the samples and information collected were brought back to the United States for analysis mainly due to the absence of appropriate scientific equipment and high-speed computers for data processing. Several discussants said that they chose this method of analysis because Russian facilities were "pathetic" or "appalling." One scientist said that they "tried to use Russian technologies as much as possible." A DOE National Laboratory representative noted: "Their scientists are top-notch," adding that while the Russian research infrastructure was "not on par with U.S. facilities, they are very functional." A number of other discussants described the Russian facilities as adequate but rapidly becoming outdated.

Russian Contributions

Although several acknowledged that it was difficult to measure the Russian contribution, in half of the cases we discussed, the Russian contribution to the collaborative work was judged to be at least equal to the U.S. contribution. Contributions were mostly in-kind. They range from use of laboratories to sharing of research materials, data, and research equipment. Several discussants noted that they "got great access" to data. Russian institutions paid the salaries for Russian scientists and technicians involved in collaborations, and transportation and lodgings were often offered to U.S. scientists. Russian assistance in obtaining visas and other government documents for travel within Russia and export of research samples and data was also acknowledged. One respondent said the cost and time required to obtain these documents could have been much higher without Russian help. In some cases, U.S. scientists reported that Russian contributions were so critical that the U.S. scientists could not otherwise have done the research or could only have done it at much higher cost. For example, the Russian institute involved in an oceanographic research project made available the use of its ice-breaking ship, which according to one scientist is "the best in the world."

Rarely were the Russian researchers able to offer a financial contribution to the project. In justifying the lack of a Russian financial contribution, one person noted, "There are a lot of talented people over there. It's a shame they have nowhere to go for funding these days." Another noted, "It is sad what has happened to Russian science in the past decade. It's been a hard time for Russian scientists."

In several cases, respondents underlined the importance of the intellectual contribution of their Russian counterparts to the project or to their conceptual understanding of the research question. One U.S. scientist involved in an ecosystems research project said, "There was a huge gap in technology but not in creativity. Those guys were incredible. I left with enormous respect for their work." Another scientist who participated in a geophysics collaborative research project remarked, "Nobody else does it better. These [Russian] researchers are by far the leaders [and] the Russians had a unique capability."

Doing research in Russia has its challenges. Some U.S. representatives reported a lack of cooperation from local officials, poor facilities, bureaucratic red tape, and a maze of domestic travel and export controls, as well as problems in communication. However, a few also noted that every dollar goes a long way in Russia when a good working relationship is present.

Necessity of Cooperation with Russia

In more than three-quarters of the projects we discussed with scientists and managers, respondents reported that the work could not have been done without collaborating with Russian counterparts. Three who said that the research *could* have been done without Russian help added that it could not have been done as well. Collaboration gave U.S. scientists access to Russian data or field sites to gather samples. For example, U.S. scientists emphasized that soil and climate data collected continuously by Russian scientists in the past decades may be the only samples of their kind in the world. Access to such information fills important gaps in what the U.S. (and world) scientific communities understand about global climate change. Another discussant reported that their project resulted in the deployment of an arctic monitoring system that could not have been done without help from Russia. U.S. representatives also reported that collaboration reduced the time required to complete the projects and Russian data and input from Russian scientists improved the quality of the research project. Finally, one U.S. scientist said, "It would be arrogant to go to Russia to do science without involving Russian scientists."

Scientific Benefits to the United States

Overwhelmingly, the representatives with whom we spoke said that there was a scientific benefit to conducting the research project in question. Respondents reported scientific benefits in 32 of the 35 projects covered in these conversations. One person said that his team was able to observe two unique techniques for treating radioactive coolants. Another said that the benefit to the United States was "huge" based upon the information he was able to access.

Project Outcomes

Several representatives noted that simply "better understanding" and a "network of colleagues" was a significant and useful outcome resulting from collaborative research. Significant new data were created in a number of cases. Training of students was also cited as a key outcome. Out of 35 project collaborations covered, at least 37 scientific publications in professional journals and books (some co-authored with Russian counterparts) were reported as having been produced. Products also included databases and Internet-based information sharing networks. Several researchers also reported excellent cooperative relationships and are continuing their collaborations with follow-on activities.

Russian S&T Capacity Benefits

As to whether these collaborations sustained or improved Russian scientific or technical capacity, our conversations with U.S. project representatives revealed a complex picture. Increased capacity was reported in 20 of the 35 projects covered in these conversations. Russian scientists built capacity as a result of direct involvement in the research project, as well as the training of Russian graduate students and visits to U.S. laboratories. Three U.S. researchers said that collaboration helped to "maintain and enhance the indigenous capacity of Russian S&T institutions outside of the military complex." Another said that collaboration "introduced [Russian scientists] to global scientific networks."

Those who did not observe increased Russian scientific or technical capacity as a result of the collaboration explained either that the project was not designed for this purpose or that some of the best Russian scientists had left Russia for work overseas or outside academia because of deterioration of the Russian economy and scientific establishment. One U.S. researcher observed a "75 to 90 percent reduction in staff in geology and geophysics institutes in Russia." Another reported that young Russian scientists are not entering his field (soil geology) because financial rewards lie in other areas such as computer science. Given the depressed state of the Russian scientific establishment, some U.S. scientists expressed the belief that Russian science should be maintained. Collaboration helps to keep Russian scientists active in their work. In addition, U.S. access to Russian databases and study samples might help to preserve valuable data and research materials. A few U.S. researchers even see a bright spot in the deterioration of the Russian/Soviet science establishment. In their view, only the most committed and able Russian scientists can survive—and those scientists are learning about the Western science system through international collaboration.

Appendix

A. Summary of S&T Data Presented in This Report

Table A.1 on the following page presents a summary of U.S. government spending on the S&T relationship with Russia, by agency.

Table A.1

U.S. Government Spending on the S&T Relationship by Agency

Agency	Types of spending (specific projects or activities)		U.S. Government research and development ($K)				U.S. Government science and technology ($K)			
			FY94	FY96	FY98	FY99	FY94	FY96	FY98	FY99
U.S. Agency for International Development	All bureaus, R&D and S&T		$30,000	$30,000	$30,000	$30,000	$5,000	$5,000	$5,000	$5,000
Department of Agriculture	All services R&D		$670	$610	$160	$120	$900	$900	$900	$900
	Special programs	Cochran Fellowship Program					$750	$750	$750	$750
		Emerging Markets Program					$150	$150	$150	$150
Department of Commerce	National Oceanographic and Atmospheric		$185	$215	$310	$330				
Department of Defense	All departments and agencies, R&D		$4,900	$3,400	$3,200	$1,800	$12,250	$12,250	$3,250	$3,250
	Special programs	Collaborative Biotechnology Programs					$2,000	$2,000	$2,000	$2,000
		Defense Enterprise Fund					$1,250	$1,250	$1,250	$1,250
		Defense Conversion Funds					$9,000	$9,000	$0	$0
Department of Energy	All offices and laboratories, R&D and S&T		$71,000	$90,000	$91,000	$72,000	$21,500	$20,500	$20,500	$20,500
	Special programs	Nuclear Cities Initiative					$2,500	$2,500	$2,500	$2,500
		Initiatives for Proliferation Prevention	$250	$1,000	$650	$440	$18,000	$18,000	$18,000	$18,000
		International Science and Technology Center	$0	$15	$220	$150	$0	$0	$0	$0
		Energy Efficiency Centers	$1,400	$760	$550	$0	$1,000	$0	$0	$0
Department of Health and Human Services	All agencies and institutes, R&D and S&T		$14,000	$14,000	$13,000	$12,000				
	Special programs	Biotechnology Engagement Program					$0	$0	$0	$0
		Training and Exchange Programs	$300	$200	$0	$0	$3,000	$2,800	$2,950	$2,500
Environmental Protection Agency							$1,000	$1,000	$1,000	$1,000
Federal Emergency Management Agency							$1,000	$1,000	$1,000	$1,000
Geological Survey										
National Aeronautical Space Administration			$172,700	$230,000	$220,000	$71,000				
National Science Foundation	All directorates, R&D		$19,000	$18,400	$20,000	$22,000				
	Special programs	Civilian R&D Foundation	$0	$0	$0	$3,100	$0	$2,500	$2,500	$2,500
Department of State	International Science and Technology Center						$8,600	$8,600	$8,600	$8,600
	Special programs	Civilian R&D Foundation					$0	$3,000	$3,000	$3,000
		Biotechnology Engagement Program					$4,000	$4,000	$4,000	$4,000
TOTALS			$312,755	$386,825	$377,670	$212,350	$57,250	$61,550	$52,700	$52,250

RAND*MR1504-T.A1*

B. Methodology Used in This Study

This appendix describes the data collection efforts used in this study. The methodology used for this study, with only minor modifications, is the same one used in four previous RAND reports (see Wagner, 1995, 1997; Wagner and Berstein, 1999; Wagner, Yezril, and Hassell, 2000).

Creating the Data Set

We consulted a number of data sources to compile information for this report. Some information on government R&D spending is electronically available through RAND's RaDiUS database (http://radius.rand.org). RaDiUS is a fully searchable data system that contains information on the more than $80 billion of annual spending classified by the federal government as "research and development," as defined by Office of Management and Budget.[1] We used this database in the first stage of data collection. Government agencies also provided information for this report and published reports were consulted for additional information.

Figure B.1 shows the five steps taken to create the initial data set for this inventory. Step 1 involved collecting data from official and primary data sources. For example, the RaDiUS database was searched using an iterative search strategy. Searches were conducted on single words (such as "Russia" in conjunction with "collaboration"), on units of government (such as "National Science Foundation"), and on countries and continents (such as "former Soviet Union"). Dozens of searches were run to capture all relevant programs, projects, and awards.

Step 2 involved examining abstracts of programs and awards. We then sorted the data and conducted additional searches where needed.

---

[1] *Research and development* is a budget term used by the Office of Management and Budget and applied within government agencies to define a specific form of federal investment activity. Office of Management and Budget Circular A-11 defines "research and development" as activities falling within three general guidelines: (1) *Basic Research*—Systematic study to gain knowledge or understanding of the fundamental aspects of phenomena and of observable facts without specific applications toward processes or products in mind. (2) *Applied Research*—Systematic study directed toward greater knowledge or understanding necessary to determine the means by which a recognized and specific need may be met. (3) *Development*—Application of knowledge toward the production of useful materials, devices, and systems, or methods, including design, development, and improvement of prototypes and new processes to meet specific requirements.

62

RAND*MR1504-B.1*

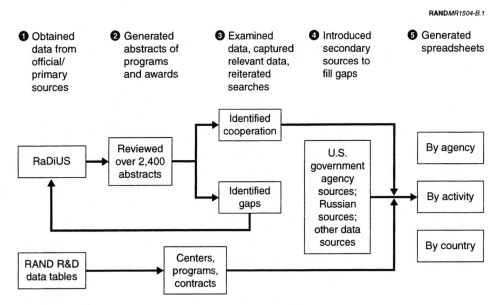

❶ Obtained data from official/ primary sources

❷ Generated abstracts of programs and awards

❸ Examined data, captured relevant data, reiterated searches

❹ Introduced secondary sources to fill gaps

❺ Generated spreadsheets

Figure B.1—Method Used to Compile Data

Step 3 of the process involved examining the set of projects and the budgetary information we had collected, identifying the relevant information, and conducting additional data searches and literature reviews where needed. Once the full set of relevant activities was identified, the project descriptions and award abstracts were sorted, coded, and classified according to a range of characteristics described below. This step also involved consultations with federal funding experts and with staff of the Office of Science and Technology Policy to identify where additional data were needed.

Step 4 of the collection effort involved contacting officials in federal government agencies who could validate the information collected or provide additional information. We also consulted earlier data collections that RAND has collated and compared these with the data set we compiled for this project: In some cases, additions were made from other data sets, and some estimates were made based on reports from agencies as well as earlier RAND studies.

Finally, step 5 in the process involved compiling all the data collected from all sources, placing the data in spreadsheets, examining the data for duplications and obvious errors, and then analyzing the data set.

Scope of the Data Collection Effort

This inventory includes any type of program-based activity—projects or awards (contract, grant, or cooperative agreement)—that has, as *one of the principal purposes*, the sponsorship of international cooperation with Russia, and multinational cooperative projects where Russia is a partner along with the United States and other nations. Project descriptions that name a Russian collaborator or a subject involving research in Russia are included. Clearly, much of the international activity, coordination, and sharing that goes on at an informal level is not captured by this inventory because we limited the study to activities for which cooperation is a specific stated project goal.

Where a project or award describes international scientific or technical cooperation with Russia as a principal part of that activity, the *full average annual* budget authority for the relevant years was included in the inventory.[2] While this method may have led to overcounting in some cases, the alternatives were unworkable.[3]

Cooperation is defined for the purposes of this study as federally supported activities in which a U.S. government-funded researcher is involved in a project with a foreign researcher, a foreign research institution, a multinational institution, or a multinational research project. Projects and awards that fell within this definition encompass scientist-to-scientist collaboration and field research in which a scientist works with a collaborator to gain access to a natural resource; research for a Ph.D. dissertation; and government agencies supporting the conduct of research through operational and technical support. The definition did not include activities for which a U.S. government official met briefly or shared data episodically with counterparts from other countries—which would generally be considered "informal" cooperation.

Agencies that use contracts, grants, and cooperative agreements to conduct most or all of their S&T activities are the most fully represented in the RaDiUS database and therefore are the most fully represented in this report. When government money changes hands, records are made of the transactions and the grant or contract recipient often provides a full description of the planned activities.[4] This is often referred to as extramural research. Agencies that emphasize extramural research include the National Science Foundation,[5] Health

---

[2]In many cases, the activities identified in this inventory were funded on a multiyear basis. In these cases, RaDiUS reports—and the project team counted—the average annual funding figure.

[3]Possible alternatives included (1) asking agency officials to report on the share of a project dedicated to R&D, data they usually do not have available; (2) contacting principal investigators directly and asking them to report on the extent of funding dedicated to cooperation with Russia, a Herculean task given the final data set of nearly 2,000 projects; or (3) having RAND staff make a judgment, an impossible task without having additional information.

[4]If international cooperation was established after the grant or contract was awarded, the activity would not be captured by this search methodology.

[5]Approximately 95 percent of NSF R&D funds leave the agency in the form of grants or contracts.

and Human Services,[6] the U.S. Department of Agriculture, and the non–lab-based activities of DOD and DOE.

When R&D is conducted within government laboratories—i.e., as intramural research—spending is more difficult to track. Although we made an effort to identify and characterize these activities, cooperative activities within government labs may not be fully represented in this study. Identifying and collecting information on intramural research involved, first, using RaDiUS to locate the likely federal agencies that conduct these activities and, second, contacting the agencies to seek the information directly. Even though we made efforts to contact agencies with program or lab-based activities, it was difficult at times to decouple the international activities from other activities going on in these agencies or laboratories. Agencies sponsoring intramural research activity include parts of NASA, EPA, USAID (through transfers to other agencies), the National Institute of Standards and Technology, DOD, DOE, and the independent Smithsonian Institution.[7]

Coding the Data

To create a useful data set for analytic purposes, the data records were classified using four main categories:

- as a binational activity, or, in cases where researchers from more than two nations are involved or where a U.S.-funded researcher reported working with Russia through a multinational research organization, as a multinational activity

- by type of cooperation, in categories developed by RAND, for identifying the character of the cooperative projects or programs funded by the U.S. federal government (see Table B.1)

- by fields of science or technology, using a list adapted by RAND from the National Science Board list of science and technology areas (see Table B.2)

- by sponsoring agency.

---

[6]Approximately 80 percent of HHS R&D funds leave the agency in the form of grants or contracts.

[7]The Smithsonian Institution is not a government agency. The institution, however, is unique in that it receives a direct line-item appropriation of R&D funds from the federal budget. These R&D funds are tracked and were included in this study.

Table B.1

Definitions of Cooperative Activity

Collaboration	A principal purpose of the research activity is to sponsor international collaboration of the following types: between a researcher funded by the U.S. government in a joint project with a collaborator from another country; when a researcher funded by the U.S. government is conducting a research program that involves actively sharing information with another researcher conducting the experimental or observational research; or when a researcher is contributing to an international cooperative project
Conference	Either foreign or domestic—including symposia, workshops, or other official meetings where scientists from around the world participate in a scientific or technical meeting to describe and share ongoing research
Database development	The U.S. government is sponsoring the creation of an international database of information being collected from sources worldwide, which will be available to researchers from around the world
Operational support	The U.S. government is funding the building, maintenance, and/or operation of an international research center in the United States or in a foreign country designed specifically for the purposes of international collaboration
Standards development	The U.S. government is sponsoring the development of a technical or scientific standard that will serve as the basis for future research, development, or production for practitioners around the world
Technology transfer	The U.S. government is actively seeking to transfer technology from a foreign country to the United States
Technical support	A U.S. government laboratory or a U.S. government-sponsored researcher is providing research and development results or other support to a foreign researcher or laboratory

Strengths and Limitations of This Approach

This data collection method has both strengths and weaknesses. It was created in large part to take advantage of RAND's RaDiUS database. RaDiUS both creates opportunities on the one hand and constrains analysis on the other. It creates opportunities because the analyst can study scientific research at its smallest unit

Table B.2

Fields of Science Used to Classify Projects

Agricultural sciences	Demography	Oceanography
Anthropology	Earth sciences	Other earth sciences
Archeology	Economics	Other engineering sciences
Atmospheric sciences	Environmental sciences	Other life sciences
Biology	Genetics	Other physical sciences
Biomedical sciences	Geography	Other social sciences
Biotechnology	Geology	Physics
Chemical engineering	Health	Plant biology
Chemistry	Materials sciences	
Computer engineering	Mathematics	

of aggregation—the research project. Groups of research projects can be aggregated into logical categories unconstrained by the views of agency officials or scientists who, if asked to self-report, might unwittingly distort activities according to privately held and untestable mental models.

The way the data are collected and reported in RaDiUS also constrains analysis. Activities supported by government and not classified as R&D (in the budgeting phenomenon described in Section 1) may well be part of the overall S&T infrastructure. These activities are not accounted for in RaDiUS, leaving the analyst able to paint part of the picture in great detail while leaving the edges of the landscape blurred. For example, a report issued by the Centers for Disease Control and Prevention and the Agency for Toxic Substance and Disease Registry, *Global Health Activities Annual Report, Fiscal Year 1998* (http://www.cdc.gov/ogh/ghar98), describes a number of international activities being conducted with Russia. Among these are neonatal screening, laboratory standardization efforts, and technology transfer for the detection of hepatitis. None of these activities are reported in RaDiUS. The activities are largely funded by USAID, with a small amount of funds provided by NIH and CDC. Agency officials at CDC cannot decouple R&D from other types of funding being committed to these projects. All of these activities have scientific components; other parts of government report similar activities as "R&D."

Moreover, the approach requires the reader to accept the categories used here rather than matching the data analysis more closely to the way that government officials think about budgeting and planning. For example, most government officials do not perceive "R&D" to be a separate activity from their overall planning and operations. Rather, each agency makes independent judgments about what to call "R&D." These judgments do not use common assumptions. Thus, it is difficult to say that all the data available are provided in equal detail or are directly comparable.

On the plus side, the data included here have been gathered from the bottom up: We identified activities at the lower levels and aggregated them into programs, bureaus, and agencies. This approach enables consistent screening of the data using a single filter created by RAND. This helps ensure the comparability of data across agencies. This approach also has the advantage of identifying cooperative activities in actual operation as opposed to cooperation proposed in international bilateral and multilateral cooperative agreements. Finally, the method we used is transparent and reproducible. This allows trend analysis over time and across agencies.[8]

Our approach also has limitations imposed by the data. Some agencies do not compile or report data on activities at the project or award level. In these cases, the inventory includes programs at higher aggregations such as budget line items. This lack of detail for the full inventory implies that the compiled data do not reflect the full spectrum of all project-level activities being funded by the U.S. government. USAID, for example, reports data only at the budget line item, so no additional analysis or comparison of USAID activities is possible. The USAID budget line-item data are delineated by region, but those data are the most detailed we could find for USAID activities. When this inventory was performed, USAID could not provide additional information on the types of R&D activities sponsored in these regions. The EPA also does not report detailed project-level activities. The Department of Defense stopped providing funding amounts for its projects, so later years cannot be tracked against earlier years or compared with other agencies. We have used estimates for most of DOD activities. Some Department of Energy and DOD lab-based activities may also be unreported.

Overall, this report contains more detailed information than would have been available before the RaDiUS database became available, and it enables a close look at specific activities. These features can be considered a net plus in understanding the operations of government and the role of government in supporting S&T. Additional research and analysis, as well as a refinement in data collection and reporting, is needed, however, because this approach still falls short of providing the government decisionmaker with the most detailed information.

---

[8]This is also the reason we used "R&D" instead of the larger set of activities that would be represented by the term "science and technology."

C. Active S&T Agreements Between the United States and Russia, 1993–2000

The following pages contain a list of U.S.-Russian S&T agreements collected by the Department of State. It was current as of the time this report was printed.

	Official Title	Start Date	End Date	Type	Renewal/Extension	S&T Agreement Content & Description
1	AGREEMENT BETWEEN THE GOVERNMENT OF THE UNITED STATES OF AMERICA AND THE GOVERNMENT OF THE RUSSIAN FEDERATION ON SCIENCE AND TECHNOLOGY COOPERATION	16-Dec-93	16-Dec-03	Umbrella	10 year agreement. May be extended for further 10-year periods by written agreement.	Umbrella agreement
2	MEMORANDUM OF UNDERSTANDING ON COOPERATION IN TELECOMMUNICATIONS	NO RECORD AT L/T	Indefinite	MOU	Indefinite	Telecommunications MOU/ITU Focus
3	STATE/FISHERIES	4-Apr-94	31-Dec-98	NO RECORD AT L/T	NO RECORD AT L/T	Expired GIFA/ Access to fisheries resources
4	AGREEMENT BETWEEN THE UNION OF SOVIET SOCIALIST REPUBLICS AND THE UNITED STATES OF AMERICA ON SCIENTIFIC AND TECHNICAL COOPERATION IN THE FIELD OF PEACEFUL USES OF ATOMIC ENERGY	1-Jun-90	1-Jun-95	Agreement	5 year agreement. May be extended by written agreement following joint review.	Four MOC's
	MEMORANDUM OF COOPERATION IN THE FIELD OF CIVILIAN NUCLEAR REACTOR SAFETY BETWEEN THE UNITED STATES OF AMERICA AND THE UNION OF SOVIET SOCIALISTS REPUBLICS	26-Apr-88	26-Apr-93	MOC	5 year agreement. May be extended by written agreement following joint review.	MOC on nuclear reactor safety
	MEMORANDUM OF COOPERATION IN THE FIELD OF MAGNETIC CONFINEMENT FUSION BETWEEN THE US DEPARTMENT OF ENERGY AND THE USSR MINISTRY OF ATOMIC POWER AND INDUSTRY	NO RECORD AT L/T	5-Jul-96	MOC	5 year agreement. May be extended by written agreement following joint review.	MOC on fundamental fusion
	MEMORANDUM OF COOPERATION IN THE FIELDS OF ENVIRONMENTAL RESTORATION AND WASTE MANAGEMENT BETWEEN THE UNITED STATES OF AMERICA AND THE UNION OF SOVIET SOCIALIST REPUBLICS	18-Sep-90	18-Sep-95	MOC	5 year agreement. May be extended by written agreement following joint review.	MOC on environmental restoration and waste management
	MEMORANDUM OF COOPERATION IN THE FIELDS OF RESEARCH ON FUNDAMENTAL PROPERTIES OF MATTER BETWEEN THE UNITED STATES DEPARTMENT OF ENERGY AND THE MINISTRY OF ATOMIC POWER AND INDUSTRY OF THE UNION OF SOVIET SOCIALIST REPUBLICS	NO RECORD AT L/T	5-Jul-96	MOC	5 year agreement. May be extended by written agreement following joint review.	MOC on research on the fundamental properties of matter
5	AGREEMENT BETWEEN THE GOVERNMENT OF THE UNITED STATES OF AMERICA AND THE GOVERNMENT OF THE RUSSIAN FEDERATION ON COOPERATION IN RESEARCH ON RADIATION EFFECTS FOR THE PURPOSE OF MINIMIZING THE CONSEQUENCES OF RADIOACTIVE CONTAMINATION ON HEALTH AND THE ENVIRONMENT	14-Jan-94	14-Jan-99	Agreement	5 year agreement. May be amended or extended by written agreement following joint review.	Cooperative research on radiation effects to minimize consequences of radioactive contamination
6	TECHNICAL COOPERATION ARRANGEMENT CONCERNING ENERGY EFFICIENCY DEMONSTRATION ZONES IN THE RUSSIAN FEDERATION BETWEEN THE DEPARTMENT OF ENERGY OF THE UNITED STATES OF AMERICA AND THE MINISTRY OF SCIENCE OF TECHNOLOGICAL POLICY AND THE MINISTRY OF FUELS AND ENERGY OF THE RUSSIAN FEDERATION	NO RECORD AT L/T	1-Oct-96	Technical Cooperation Arrangement	3 year agreement. May be extended by written agreement.	Cooperation on energy efficiency and renewable energy technologies

	Official Title	Start Date	End Date	Type	Renewal/Extension	S&T Agreement Content & Description
7	AN AGREEMENT BETWEEN THE GOVERNMENT OF THE UNITED STATES OF AMERICA AND THE GOVERNMENT OF THE RUSSIAN FEDERATION FOR COOPERATION IN THE GLOBE PROGRAM	16-Dec-94	15-Dec-00	Agreement	Automatically renewing every 5 years.	GLOBE program on environmental science
8	AGREEMENT BETWEEN THE GOVERNMENT OF THE UNITED STATES OF AMERICA AND THE GOVERNMENT OF THE UNION OF SOVIET SOCIALIST REPUBLICS ON COOPERATION IN OCEAN STUDIES	1-Jun-90	31-May-00	Agreement	5 year agreement. May be amended or extended by written agreement.	Ocean studies agreement
9	AGREEMENT BETWEEN THE GOVERNMENT OF THE UNITED STATES OF AMERICA AND THE GOVERNMENT OF THE RUSSIAN FEDERATION ON COOPERATION IN THE FIELD OF PROTECTION OF THE ENVIRONMENT AND NATURAL RESOURCES	23-Jun-94	23-Jun-99	Agreement	Automatically renewing every 5 years.	Atmosphere, water, soil, arctic, coastal, marine impact of environmental factors on human health
10	MEMORANDUM OF UNDERSTANDING BETWEEN THE DEPARTMENT OF DEFENSE OF THE UNITED STATES OF AMERICA AND THE MINISTRY OF DEFENSE AND THE MINISTRY OF SCIENCE AND TECHNOLOGY POLICY OF THE RUSSIAN FEDERATION ON SCIENTIFIC AND TECHNICAL COOPERATION IN ACOUSTIC THERMOMETRY OF OCEAN CLIMATE	16-Dec-94	15-Dec-99	MOU	5 year agreement. May be extended by written agreement.	MOD/MIST MOU in acoustic thermometry spatially averaged temperatures in ocean climates
11	USDA/ARS	NO RECORD AT L/T	Indefinite		NO RECORD AT L/T	Scientific research and exchange in agriculture, food and natural resources
12	MEMORANDUM OF UNDERSTANDING BETWEEN THE FOREST SERVICE OF THE UNITED STATES DEPARTMENT OF AGRICULTURE AND THE FEDERAL FOREST SERVICE OF RUSSIA ON COOPERATION IN THE FIELD OF FORESTRY	13-May-94	12-May-99	MOU	Automatically renewing every 5 years.	Forest regeneration, protection, sustainable development, conservation and management
13	USDA/USFS	NO RECORD AT L/T	Indefinite	NO RECORD AT L/T	NO RECORD AT L/T	RAS MOU modeling global climate change
14	MEMORANDUM OF UNDERSTANDING BETWEEN THE DEPARTMENT OF TRANSPORTATION OF THE UNITED STATES OF AMERICA AND THE MINISTRY OF TRANSPORTATION OF THE RUSSIAN FEDERATION ON COOPERATION IN TRANSPORTATION SCIENCE AND TECHNOLOGY	23-Jun-94	22-Jun-99	MOU	5 year agreement. May be extended by written agreement.	MOT/MOU on civil aviation, highways, railroads, air traffic control, river transport, port technologies
15	AGREEMENT BETWEEN THE UNITED STATES OF AMERICA AND THE UNION OF SOVIET SOCIALIST REPUBLICS ON COOPERATION IN ARTIFICIAL HEART RESEARCH AND DEVELOPMENT	28-Jun-74	28-Jun-99	Agreement	Automatically renewing every 5 years.	NHLBI MOU on cardiological research and artificial heart technologies

	Official Title	Start Date	End Date	Type	Renewal/Extension	S&T Agreement Content & Description
16	MEMORANDUM OF UNDERSTANDING ON COOPERATION IN THE FIELD OF BASIC BIOMEDICAL RESEARCH BETWEEN THE NATIONAL INSTITUTES OF HEALTH OF THE UNITED STATES OF AMERICA AND THE ACADEMY OF SCIENCES OF THE RUSSIAN FEDERATION	23-Jun-94	22-Jun-99	MOU	5 year agreement. May be amended or extended by written agreement.	NIH cooperative research on immunology, cancer, genetics, neurobiology, molecular biology, AIDS
17	AGREEMENT BETWEEN THE GOVERNMENT OF THE UNITED STATES OF AMERICA AND THE GOVERNMENT OF THE RUSSIAN FEDERATION ON COOPERATION IN THE FIELDS OF PUBLIC HEALTH AND BIOMEDICAL RESEARCH	14-Jan-94	14-Jan-99	Agreement	5 year agreement. May be amended or extended by written agreement.	Cooperative biomedical and public health research on disease control and prevention
18	MEMORANDUM OF UNDERSTANDING BETWEEN THE FOOD AND DRUG ADMINISTRATION PUBLIC HEALTH SERVICE DEPARTMENT OF HEALTH AND HUMAN SERVICES OF THE UNITED STATES OF AMERICA AND THE MINISTRY OF HEALTH AND MEDICAL INDUSTRY AND THE STATE COMMITTEE FOR SANITARY AND EPIDEMOLOGICAL SURVEILLANCE OF THE RUSSIAN FEDERATION CONCERNING COOPERATION AND INFORMATION EXCHANGE ON DRUGS AND BIOLOGICAL PRODUCTS FACILITATING IMPORTATION	NO RECORD AT L/T	15-Feb-97	MOU	3 year agreement. May be extended by written agreement.	Information exchange on drugs and biological products
19	MEMORANDUM OF UNDERSTANDING ON SCIENTIFIC AND TECHNICAL COOPERATION IN THE FIELDS OF STANDARDS AND METROLOGY BETWEEN THE US NATIONAL INSTITUTE OF STANDARDS AND TECHNOLOGY AND THE STATE COMMITTEE OF THE RUSSIAN FEDERATION FOR STANDARDIZATION, METROLOGY, AND CERTIFICATION	23-Mar-93	22-Mar-98	MOU	5 year agreement. May be amended or extended by written agreement.	MOU with GOSSTANDART on standardization
20	MEMORANDUM OF UNDERSTANDING BETWEEN THE US NATIONAL INSTITUTE OF STANDARDS AND TECHNOLOGY AND THE USSR ACADEMY OF SCIENCES ON COOPERATION IN THE PHYSICAL, CHEMICAL AND ENGINEERING SCIENCES	13-May-91	12-May-96	MOU	5 year agreement. May be amended or extended by written agreement.	RAS MOU on physical, engineering, and chemical sciences
21	MEMORANDUM OF UNDERSTANDING BETWEEN THE UNITED STATES OF AMERICA AND THE RUSSIAN FEDERATION ON THE GLOBAL INFORMATION INFRASTRUCTURE INITIATIVE	NO RECORD AT L/T	Indefinite	MOU	Indefinite	Cooperative projects with FCC/MoT in developing global information infrastructure GII
22	DOI/BLM	14-May-92	14-May-97	NO RECORD AT L/T	NO RECORD AT L/T	Satellite monitoring of five paired
23	MEMORANDUM OF UNDERSTANDING ON COOPERATION IN THE FIELDS OF MINING RESEARCH AND MINERALS INFORMATION BETWEEN THE UNITED STATES BUREAU OF MINES OF THE DEPARTMENT OF INTERIOR OF THE UNITED STATES OF AMERICA AND MOSCOW STATE MINING UNIVERSITY OF THE RUSSIAN FEDERATION	16-Dec-93	16-Dec-98	MOU	5 year agreement. May be extended by written agreement.	Cooperation with Moscow State Mining University, mine safety, mining sciences, minerals research, minerals processing and reclamation technologies

	Official Title	Start Date	End Date	Type	Renewal/Extension	S&T Agreement Content & Description
24	CONVENTION BETWEEN THE UNITED STATES OF AMERICA AND THE UNION OF SOVIET SOCIALIST REPUBLICS CONCERNING THE CONSERVATION OF MIGRATORY BIRDS AND THEIR ENVIRONMENTS	NO RECORD AT L/T	Indefinite	NO RECORD AT L/T	Indefinite	Cooperative MOU with EnvMin on migratory bird research and protection technologies
25	MEMORANDUM OF UNDERSTANDING BETWEEN THE MINERALS MANAGEMENT SERVICE OF THE DEPARTMENT OF INTERIOR OF THE UNITED STATES OF AMERICA AND THE COMMITTEE OF THE RUSSIAN FEDERATION ON GEOLOGY AND USE OF UNDERGROUND RESOURCES	NO RECORD AT L/T	22-Jun-99	MOU	5 year agreement. May be amended or extended by written agreement.	Cooperation on earth sciences with RF committee on geology, risk and resources analyses
26	MEMORANDUM OF UNDERSTANDING ON COOPERATION IN THE MAPPING SCIENCES BETWEEN THE US GEOLOGICAL SURVEY OF THE DEPARTMENT OF INTERIOR OF THE UNITED STATES OF AMERICA AND THE USSR COMMITTEE OF GEODESY AND CARTOGRAPHY	14-May-91	14-May-96	MOU	Renewable every 5 years through exchange of diplomatic notes	Cooperative mapping project and services with RF Geodesy and Cartography services
27	MEMORANDUM OF UNDERSTANDING ON COOPERATION IN GEOSCIENCE BETWEEN THE US GEOLOGICAL SURVEY OF THE DEPARTMENT OF INTERIOR OF THE UNITED STATES OF AMERICA AND THE COMMITTEE ON GEOLOGY AND THE USE OF UNDERGROUND RESOURCES OF THE RUSSIAN FEDERATION AND THE ACADEMY OF SCIENCES OF THE RUSSIAN FEDERATION	23-Jun-94	22-Jun-99	MOU	Automatically renewing every 5 years.	Cooperation with ROSKOMNEDRA and RAS on basic geophysics, geochemistry, mineralogy, marine geosciences, stratigraphy, paleontology, and minerals
28	METEOR-3/TOMS IMPLEMENTING AGREEMENT BETWEEN THE NATIONAL AERONAUTICS AND SPACE ADMINISTRATION OF THE UNITED STATES OF AMERICA AND THE SENATE COMMITTEE FOR HYDROMETEOROLOGY OF THE UNION OF SOVIET SOCIALIST REPUBLICS	24-Aug-90	Indefinite	Agreement	Indefinite	Total Ozone Mapping Spectrometer RF launch 8/91
29	MEMORANDUM OF UNDERSTANDING ON COOPERATION IN FUNDAMENTAL AERONAUTICAL SCIENCES BETWEEN THE NATIONAL AERONAUTICS AND SPACE ADMINISTRATION OF THE UNITED STATES OF AMERICA AND THE STATE COMMITTEE FOR THE DEFENSE BRANCHES OF INDUSTRY OF THE RUSSIAN FEDERATION	16-Dec-93	16-Dec-98	MOU	5 year agreement. May be extended by written agreement.	Cooperative MOU with GOSKOMOBORON-PROM on fundamental aeronautical sciences, thermal protection, turbulence, composite structures, and hypersonic technologies
30	NASA/SPACE	25-Feb-94	28-Feb-04	NO RECORD AT L/T	NO RECORD AT L/T	RAS/MOU applied space geodesy to basic earth sciences research and global climate change
31	IMPLEMENTING AGREEMENT BETWEEN THE UNITED STATES NATIONAL AERONAUTICS AND SPACE ADMINISTRATION AND THE RUSSIAN SPACE AGENCY OF THE RUSSIAN FEDERATION ON HUMAN SPACE FLIGHT COOPERATION	29-Apr-93	29-Apr-98	Implementing Agreement	In force for 5 years or until completion of activities, whichever occurs first	Cooperation with RSA on shuttle-MIR Program
32	NASA/SPACE	23-Jun-94	Indefinite	NO RECORD AT L/T	NO RECORD AT L/T	Cooperation with RSA on research and development of the international space station

	Official Title	Start Date	End Date	Type	Renewal/Extension	S&T Agreement Content & Description
33	MEMORANDUM OF UNDERSTANDING BETWEEN THE NATIONAL AERONAUTICS AND SPACE ADMINISTRATION OF THE UNITED STATES OF AMERICA AND THE MINISTRY OF SCIENCE AND TECHNOLOGY POLICY OF THE RUSSIAN FEDERATION AND THE RUSSIAN SPACE AGENCY ON COOPERATION RELATING TO THE SPACE BIOMEDICAL CENTER FOR TRAINING AND RESEARCH IN THE RUSSIAN FEDERATION	30-Jun-95	30-Jun-00	MOU	5 year agreement. May be amended or extended by written agreement.	Space biomedical research facility in Moscow
34	AGREEMENT BETWEEN THE UNITED STATES OF AMERICA AND THE RUSSIAN FEDERATION CONCERNING COOPERATION IN THE EXPLORATION AND USE OF OUTER SPACE FOR PEACEFUL PURPOSES	17-Jun-92	17-Jun-97	Agreement	Renewable every 5 years through exchange of diplomatic notes	Cooperation on the peaceful uses of outer space, space biology, medicine, solar system exploration, astronomy and astrophysics, solar terrestrial physics and earth sciences [includes MARS probe]
35	MEMORANDUM OF UNDERSTANDING ON BASIC SCIENTIFIC RESEARCH COOPERATION BETWEEN THE NATIONAL SCIENCE FOUNDATION OF THE UNITED STATES OF AMERICA AND THE ACADEMY OF SCIENCES OF THE RUSSIAN FEDERATION	23-Jun-94	22-Jun-99	MOU	Renewable every 5 years	Basic cooperation MOU with RAS on all branches of science excluding clinical medical and business
36	MEMORANDUM OF COOPERATION IN THE FIELD OF CIVILIAN NUCLEAR REACTOR SAFETY BETWEEN THE UNITED STATES OF AMERICA AND THE UNION OF SOVIET SOCIALIST REPUBLICS	NO RECORD AT L/T	26-Apr-93	MOC		General information exchange
	NRC/NUCLEAR SAFETY	6-Apr-95	31-Aug-97	NO RECORD AT L/T	NO RECORD AT L/T	Thermal-hydraulic CAMP operation
	NRC/NUCLEAR SAFETY	31-Jan-95	30-Jan-00	NO RECORD AT L/T	NO RECORD AT L/T	NRC/NAS-IBRAE agreement on developing nuclear safety analysis codes
37	AGREEMENT BETWEEN THE GOVERNMENT OF THE UNITED STATES OF AMERICA AND THE GOVERNMENT OF THE RUSSIAN FEDERATION ON SCIENTIFIC AND TECHNICAL COOPERATION IN THE FIELDS OF FUELS AND ENERGY	17-Jun-92	17-Jun-97	Agreement	5 year agreement. May be amended or extended by written agreement.	Energy development agreement on cooperation in energy data exchange. Energy and ecology, fossil energy sources, electric power, energy conservation, and renewable energy sources
38	MEMORANDUM OF COOPERATION IN THE FIELD OF FOSSIL ENERGY BETWEEN THE UNITED STATES DEPARTMENT OF ENERGY AND THE RUSSIAN FEDERATION MINISTRY OF FUELS AND ENERGY	NO RECORD AT L/T	2-Sep-98	MOC	5 year agreement. May be amended or extended by written agreement following joint review.	Cooperation in the field of fossil energy technology, research, environmental assessment
39	IMPLEMENTING AGREEMENT BETWEEN THE UNITED STATES NATIONAL AERONAUTICS AND SPACE ADMINISTRATION AND THE RUSSIAN SPACE AGENCY ON NASA PARTICIPATION IN THE RUSSIAN SPECTRUM-X-GAMMA MISSION	NO RECORD AT L/T	30-Jun-00	Implementing Agreement	Automatic termination upon completion of activities	Spectrum-X-Gamma mission

	Official Title	Start Date	End Date	Type	Renewal/Extension	S&T Agreement Content & Description
40	AGREEMENT BETWEEN THE GOVERNMENT OF THE UNITED STATES OF AMERICA AND THE GOVERNMENT OF THE RUSSIAN FEDERATION ON COOPERATION IN THE PREVENTION OF POLLUTION OF THE ENVIRONMENT IN THE ARCTIC	16-Dec-94	16-Dec-99	Agreement	5 year agreement. May be extended by written agreement.	Pollution prevention, reduction, control in the Arctic
41	AGREEMENT BETWEEN THE GOVERNMENT OF THE UNITED STATES OF AMERICA AND THE GOVERNMENT OF THE UNION OF SOVIET SOCIALIST REPUBLICS CONCERNING COOPERATION IN COMBATING POLLUTION IN THE BERING AND CHUKCHI SEAS IN EMERGENCY SITUATIONS	17-Aug-89	Indefinite	Agreement	Indefinite	Emergency assistance in the event of pollution incident
42	AGREEMENT BETWEEN THE GOVERNMENT OF THE UNITED STATES OF AMERICA AND THE GOVERNMENT OF THE RUSSIAN FEDERATION REGARDING COOPERATION TO FACILITATE THE PROVISION OF ASSISTANCE	4-Apr-92	Indefinite	Agreement	Indefinite	Cooperation in facilitating the provision of humanitarian and technical assistance in support of market economic and democratic reform to benefit the Russian Federation
43	AGREEMENT BETWEEN THE GOVERNMENT OF THE UNITED STATES OF AMERICA AND THE GOVERNMENT OF THE RUSSIAN FEDERATION CONCERNING OPERATIONAL SAFETY ENHANCEMENTS, RISK EDUCATION MEASURES, AND NUCLEAR SAFETY REGULATION FOR CIVIL NUCLEAR FACILITIES IN THE RUSSIAN FEDERATION	16-Dec-93	16-Dec-98	Agreement	5 year agreement. May be extended by written agreement.	Develop emergency operating procedures, reducing risks associated with nuclear reactor operation, improve nuclear radiation standards and regulations for use in the Russian Federation
44	AGREEMENT BETWEEN THE GOVERNMENT OF THE UNITED STATES OF AMERICA AND THE GOVERNMENT OF THE RUSSIAN FEDERATION ON COOPERATION AND MUTUAL ASSISTANCE IN CUSTOMS MATTERS	28-Sep-94	28-Sep-99	Agreement	Indefinite	Information exchange on customs laws enforcement
45	AGREEMENT BETWEEN THE GOVERNMENTS OF THE UNITED STATES OF AMERICA AND THE RUSSIAN FEDERATION CONCERNING THE PROCEDURE FOR THE CUSTOMS DOCUMENTATION AND DUTY-FREE ENTRY OF GOODS TRANSPORTED WITH THE FRAMEWORK OF THE US-RUSSIAN COOPERATION IN THE EXPLORATION AND USE OF SPACE FOR PEACEFUL PURPOSES	26-Aug-96	26-Aug-01	Agreement	Renewable every 5 years through exchange of diplomatic notes	NASA/RSA goods associated with joint space partnership customs documentation and duty-free entry
Post-1995						
1	MEMORANDUM OF UNDERSTANDING BETWEEN THE NATIONAL INSTITUTE OF STANDARDS AND TECHNOLOGY OF THE DEPARTMENT OF COMMERCE OF THE UNITED STATES OF AMERICA AND THE ACADEMY OF SCIENCES OF THE RUSSIAN FEDERATION FOR SCIENTIFIC AND TECHNICAL COOPERATION IN THE PHYSICAL, CHEMICAL, AND ENGINEERING SCIENCES	16-Jul-96	16-Jul-01	MOU	5 year agreement. May be amended or extended by written agreement.	MOU on cooperation in the field of physics, chemistry, and engineering sciences

	Official Title	Start Date	End Date	Type	Renewal/Extension	S&T Agreement Content & Description
2	MEMORANDUM OF UNDERSTANDING BETWEEN THE NATIONAL SCIENCE FOUNDATION OF THE UNITED STATES OF AMERICA AND THE STATE COMMITTEE FOR SCIENCE AND TECHNOLOGY OF THE RUSSIAN FEDERATION ON COOPERATION IN HIGH PERFORMANCE SCIENTIFIC COMPUTING	7-Feb-97	7-Feb-02	MOU	agreement in force for 5 years or the duration of the S & T umbrella agreement, whichever is shorter	MOU on high performance computing
3	MEMORANDUM OF UNDERSTANDING ON BASIC SCIENTIFIC RESEARCH COOPERATION BETWEEN THE NATIONAL SCIENCE FOUNDATION OF THE UNITED STATES OF AMERICA AND THE RUSSIAN FOUNDATION FOR BASIC RESEARCH	7-Feb-97	7-Feb-02	MOU	Automatically renewing every 5 years.	Cooperation in basic scientific research

D. Protocol of Discussions with Project Representatives

1. What area of science would you say this project falls under?

2. Collaborative efforts come in several forms. Of those, we would like to know if you consider this effort to be one of the following, and let me give you some choices:

   - Collaboration in which a researcher funded by the U.S. government is working jointly with a Russian collaborator

   - Research about Russia that does not involve collaborative efforts with Russian scientists

   - Technical support in which a U.S. government laboratory or other U.S. government-sponsored researcher is providing R&D results or other support to the Russian researcher or laboratory

   - Database development in which the U.S. government is sponsoring the creation of an international database of information being collected from sources worldwide.

3. Did the research take place mainly in the United States, mainly in Russia, or equally in Russia and the U.S.?

   - If any research took place in Russia, were the Russian facilities adequate to complete the tasks?

4. Did the Russian collaborator or his/her research institution or other Russian entity make an in-kind or financial contribution to the project?

   - If there was a Russian contribution, what was that?

   - If there was no Russian contribution, why was that?

5. Was the Russian contribution less than, equal to, or more than the U.S. contribution?

6. Could this project have been done without cooperation with Russia?

7. Was there a scientific benefit to the United States that accrued as a result of participating in this project?

8. Can you point to a specific outcome that developed from this cooperation? Examples include patents, publications, or products.

9. Did the research help to build Russian scientific or technical capacity?

10. Do you have any additional comments you would like to offer?

Bibliography

American Association for the Advancement of Science, *Congressional Action on Research and Development in the FY2001 Budget*, Washington, D.C.: AAAS, 2000.

Boesman, William C., "Science and Technology in the Former Soviet Union: Capabilities and Needs," in Richard Kaufman and John P. Hart, eds., *The Former Soviet Union in Transition*, Armonk, N.Y.: M.E. Sharpe, 1993.

Carnegie Endowment for International Peace, Russian and Eurasian Program, *An Agenda for Renewal: U.S.-Russian Relations*, Washington, D.C.: CEIP, 2000.

Centers for Disease Control and Prevention, *Global Health Activities Annual Report, Fiscal Year 1998.* Available at http://www.cdc.gov/ogh/ghar98.

Frankel, Mark S., and Jane Cave, eds., *Evaluating Science and Scientists: An East-West Dialogue on Research Evaluation in Post-Communist Europe*, Budapest: Central European University Press, 1997.

General Accounting Office, Resources, Community, and Economic Development Division, *Federal Research: Information on International Science and Technology Agreements*, Washington, D.C.: Government Printing Office, GAO/RCED-99-108, April 1999.

Gokhberg, Leonid, *Russia: A Science and Technology Profile*, London: The British Council, 1999.

Gokhberg, Leonid. and Irina Kuznetsova, *Technological Innovation in Russia*, Moscow: Centre for Science Research and Statistics, 1998.

International Science and Technology Center (ISTC), *Year 2000 Review of the ISTC.* Available at http://www.istc.ru/istc/website.nsf/7d053b260fc5617bc3256a63005bd74c/over.htm.

Leiter, Sharon, *Prospects for Russian Military R&D*, Santa Monica, Calif.: RAND, MR-709-A, 1996.

National Research Council, Committee on Science, Technology, and Health Aspects of the Foreign Policy Agenda of the United States, *The Pervasive Role of Science, Technology, and Health in Foreign Policy: Imperatives for the Department of State*, Washington, D.C.: National Academy Press, 1999.

National Research Council, Office of Central Europe and Eurasia, *Partners on the Frontier: U.S.-Russian Cooperation in Science and Technology*, Proceedings of a Workshop, October 28, 1997, Washington, D.C.: National Academy Press, 1998.

National Science Board, *Science and Engineering Indicators—2000*, Arlington, Va.: National Science Foundation, NSB-00-1, 2000.

National Science Foundation, *International Dimensions of NSF Research and Education FY1997 Report*, Washington, D.C.: National Science Foundation, 1998.

Organisation for Economic Co-operation and Development, *Science and Technology Statistics in the Partners in Transition Countries and the Russian Federation*, Paris: OECD, 1996.

Organisation for Economic Co-operation and Development, Centre for Co-operation with Non-members, Directorate for Science, Technology, and Industry, *Science and Technology Main Indicators and Basic Statistics in the Russian Federation, 1992–1997*, Paris: OECD, 1999.

Schweitzer, Glenn E., *Experiments in Cooperation: Assessing U.S.-Russian Programs in Science and Technology*, New York: The Twentieth Century Fund Press, 1997.

U.S. Agency for International Development (USAID), *U.S. Assistance and Economic Cooperation Strategy for Russia*, February 1995. Available at http://www.usaid.gov/countries/ru/rus-fin.txt.

___, *FY2001 Congressional Presentation*, 2001a. Available at http://www.usaid.gov/country/ee/ru

___, *Russia:: FY 2001 Program Description and Activity Data Sheets*, 2001b. Available at http://www.usaid.gov/pubs/bj2001/ee/ru/ru_ads.html.

___, *USAID Climate Change Initiative 1998–2002*, at http://www.usaid.gov/environment/pubs/cci_usaidgec.pdf.

U.S. Department of State, *U.S. Government Assistance to and Cooperative Activities with the New Independent States of the Former Soviet Union, FY2000 Annual Report*, Washington, D.C., January 2001.

U.S. Geological Survey (USGS), *FY1998 Annual Report on USG Assistance to and Cooperative Activities with the Newly Independent States (NIS) of the Former Soviet Union* (unpblished draft submitted to the Departments of State and Interior).

___, *Overview of U.S. Geological Survey Activities in the Russian Federation*, June 29, 2001.

Wagner, Caroline S., *Techniques and Methods for Assessing the International Standings of U.S. Science*, Santa Monica, Calif.: RAND, MR-706.0-OSTP, 1995.

___, *International Cooperation in Research and Development: An Inventory of U.S. Government Spending and a Framework for Measuring Benefits*, Santa Monica, Calif.: RAND, MR-900-OSTP, 1997.

Wagner, Caroline S., and Nurith Berstein, *U.S. Government Funding of Cooperative Research and Development in North America,* Santa Monica, Calif.: RAND, MR-1115-OSTP, 1999.

Wagner, Caroline S., Irene Brahmakulam, Brian Jackson, Anny Wong, and Tatsuro Yoda, *Science and Technology Collaboration: Building Capacity in Developing Countries?* Santa Monica, Calif.: RAND, MR-1357.0-WB, 2001.

Wagner, Caroline S., Linda Staheli, James Kadtke, Edward H. Silber, and Anny Wong, *Linking Effectively: International Cooperation in Research and Development,* Santa Monica, Calif.: RAND, DB-345-OSTP, forthcoming.

Wagner, Caroline S., Allison Yezril, and Scott Hassell, *International Cooperation in Research and Development: An Update to an Inventory of U.S. Government Spending,* Santa Monica, Calif.: RAND, MR-1248-OSTP, 2000.

Zitt, Michael, Elise Bassecoulard, and Yoshiko Okubo, "Shadows of the Past in International Cooperation: Collaboration Profiles of the Top Five Producers of Science," *Scientometrics,* Vol. 47, No. 3, 2000, pp. 627–657.